W9-BGI-559

mjf

Publisher's Note: This publication is designed to provide accurate and authoritative information in regard to the subject matter covered. It is sold with the understanding that the publisher is not engaged in rendering psychological, financial, legal, or other professional services. If expert assistance or counseling is needed, the services of a competent professional should be sought.

Published by MJF Books
Fine Communications
Two Lincoln Square
60 West 66th Street
New York, NY 10023

Change Your Mind, Change Your Life
LC Control Number 00-135987
ISBN 1-56731-447-3

This edition published by arrangement with New Harbinger Publications, Inc.
This book was previously published under the title of *Prisoners of Belief*.

Manufactured in the United States of America on acid-free paper

MJF Books and the MJF colophon are trademarks of Fine Creative Media, Inc.

10 9 8 7 6 5 4 3 2 1

CHANGE YOUR MIND, CHANGE YOUR LIFE

Rebuilding Your Core Beliefs

(previously published as *Prisoners of Belief*)

MATTHEW MCKAY, PH.D. &
PATRICK FANNING

MJF BOOKS
NEW YORK

For Michael—May you never be a prisoner.

PF

For Jude—Always the one.

MM

Table of Contents

Introduction

In 1985, a fifteen-year-old girl murdered her high school classmate in Orinda, California. The community was shocked. The murdered girl had been one of the most popular and high-achieving students in the school. She was a star.

When interviewed after her crime, the teenage murderess described deep feelings of jealousy toward her victim. Most families in this upper-middle-class suburb were better off than hers — they could afford nicer houses, cars, clothes, vacations, tennis clubs, sailing lessons, and so on. She never felt like she belonged. She felt humiliated by her family's lifestyle and economic status. She was a zero, a nothing. She felt invisible in a community where everyone else seemed confident, happy, and well-heeled.

The belief that she was nothing without the trappings of wealth and status fueled enormous pain in this young woman. And the pain grew until it spilled out in an act of violence that was, very simply, a massive defense against a profound belief in her own worthlessness.

By contrast, James Baldwin grew up in the crush of ghetto poverty. Harlem was a paralyzing place, whose citizens coped with their despair with drugs and anger and dreams of escape. Hemmed in by the economics of racism, many were justified in the belief that they were helpless. Somehow, Baldwin came to see himself differently. He believed he had something to say and the ability to say it. He believed someone would listen. He believed he had the power to control his fate. Baldwin's book, *Go Tell It on the Mountain,* made an enormous contribution to understanding what it means to be poor and black in urban America.

What explains the choices made by Baldwin and the jealous teenager? How do people take such different paths? Is it enough to say that Baldwin was extremely talented? Or that the teenager was sociopathic? Or that they were both simply products of conditioning?

We will argue that the defining variable is belief. For *whatever* reason, the teenager *believed* she was nothing. Baldwin *believed* he had an important story to tell. Each was driven and defined by belief. And in the end, it is belief that either saves or crushes everyone.

Your most deeply held, core beliefs are the bedrock of your personality. They describe you as worthy or worthless, competent or incompetent, powerful or helpless, loved or scorned, self-reliant or dependent, belonging or outcast, trusting or suspicious, flexible or judgmental, secure or threatened, fairly treated or victimized.

This book is called *Prisoners of Belief* because that's what often happens — people are imprisoned by their own negative, restrictive beliefs about themselves and their world. They surround themselves with bars of conviction: "Don't try that, it's dangerous...He doesn't know I exist, I'm nothing to him...Love never lasts anyway, it's better to not get involved...I'll keep quiet, my opinion isn't worth much...Better stick to this job, I couldn't handle any more responsibility."

At the very least, this book will teach you how to shift the bars of belief slightly, to move them outward and increase the size and comfort of your prison. But with perseverance, you can shift the bars so far that they create doorways to a freer, more satisfying life.

Who Can Use This Book

You can use this book on your own to uncover, explore, test, and confirm or modify your core beliefs. The book contains everything you'll need in the way of detailed explanations, examples, and step-by-step exercises.

What this book can't provide is feedback and support tailored to your unique history and circumstances. For that, a good friend, supportive spouse, or willing therapist can be invaluable.

If you are a helping professional doing cognitive behavioral work, this book will serve as a useful text to share with your clients and will provide a clear model for applying some of the more recent advances in cognitive theory.

Who Should *Not* Use This Book

Victims of child abuse. Working with core beliefs requires that you relive some of your earliest traumatic experiences. If you were physically, emotionally, or sexually abused as a child, the memories that will be aroused can be very painful and upsetting. You should use this book only under the supervision of a mental health professional.

Those in crisis. Core belief work is a *long-term* solution to *chronic* emotional and behavioral problems. If you are in an *acute* crisis situation — especially if you are deeply depressed or contemplating suicide — you should seek immediate help from a mental health professional. When your mood and situation stabilize, ask your therapist about working on core beliefs with this book.

People struggling with addictions. If you consume a lot of alcohol or drugs, or if you have an eating disorder, you should work on those problems first with a professional.

Those lacking self-motivation. Exploring and modifying core beliefs takes time and commitment. If you know that you have a hard time getting yourself going and keeping yourself moving toward self-improvement, stack the deck in your favor from the outset. Take this book to a helping professional who is well versed in cognitive behavioral techniques and enlist his or her aid.

How To Use This Book

It's fine to skip around in this book to see what's coming up. But do the exercises in the order given. The chapters follow a logical progression, each building on the one before.

Chapter 1 explains how core beliefs are the basis of the rules you live by, how those rules color your inner monologue, and how the whole system is maintained by confirmatory bias and mental grooving. Chapter 2 offers two methods of identifying your core beliefs: the Core Beliefs Inventory and the Monologue Diary.

Chapter 3 helps you explore both the positive and negative consequences of your core beliefs. In chapter 4 you choose a belief with predominantly negative consequences and methodically review your history, looking for evidence supporting or disproving the belief.

Chapter 5 guides you in uncovering the rules for living derived from your core beliefs. Then chapter 6 shows you how to objectively test some of the more restrictive rules in real life. When you prove to your own satisfaction that a rule is invalid, it allows you to shift the underlying core belief.

Chapter 7 tells how to derive new rules from your revised core beliefs and how to gradually put those rules into action in more and more areas of your life. Chapter 8 concludes the book with detailed instructions for visualizing important scenes from the past in light of your changed core beliefs. In imagination, you comfort your inner child and have an opportunity to actually rewrite your psychological history.

A Final Caution

It's easy to read this book. It's short and simple to understand. But mere reading is not enough to affect core beliefs. Results will come only from doing the exercises in the book, not from comprehending the concepts. So *do the exercises.* There is no substitute for the *process* of uncovering and testing your beliefs. No change can happen without it.

Be patient. It's taken a lifetime to form your unique blend of core beliefs. It will probably take several months to affect your beliefs in any way.

Be cautious. Some self-help books offer a superficial quick fix, akin to slapping a coat of paint on the front of a collapsing building. This is a different kind of book. We are proposing some deep and serious work — more like making major repairs to a building's foundation. You will be applying some enormously powerful techniques to the very foundation of your identity. Proceed carefully, one step at a time. Give yourself enough time to fully understand the directions and absorb the results of each exercise.

And finally, be skeptical. We don't expect you to change what you believe about yourself just because it has some negative consequences or because you might arguably be "happier" if you believed something else. The fact is, you believe what you believe for some very real reasons. Don't change your beliefs in the slightest until you become *convinced* that something else is true.

Matthew McKay
Patrick Fanning
Calistoga, California, January 1991

1

Your Self-Portrait

Your core beliefs are the basic concepts you live by. They form your picture of yourself, a portrait of your flaws and strengths, your abilities, your worth, and your relationship to the world.

Your core beliefs are your identity. They define how you feel about yourself, the emotional tone of your life. They influence everything, from whom you choose as a spouse to whether you deserve the pleasure of a long hot bath. They establish the limits of what you can achieve. They determine who you feel worthy to pursue for friendship. They define what you can expect from life in the form of nourishment, satisfaction, and emotional well-being.

Consider Simon. Since childhood, he has seen himself as flawed and unworthy. To compensate, he has worked hard to construct an acceptable facade: tailored suits, expensive jewelry, a modulated speaking voice, a firm handshake, a warm smile. But he is convinced that anyone who comes to know him intimately will see through the manicured exterior to the frightened, empty person underneath. Because of his unworthiness, Simon feels like an impostor. He has decided that he can't risk getting close, that the sense of loneliness and deprivation that he feels must continue. No one who really knew him, he thinks, could ever feel love.

Or consider Carmen. She sees herself as incompetent: "Nothing I do works. I make incredibly lousy decisions. Even if

I make the right decision, I screw it up so things fall apart." So Carmen has become passive. She drifts, allowing events to carry her along. She accepts the attention of uncaring, even brutal men. She stays at a stressful, low-paying job because "I'd probably end up someplace worse." She lives with her abusive grandmother because "I don't know if I could take care of myself."

Clearly, your self-portrait is the basis of most major life decisions. It sets your sights and establishes your basic fears. When a portrait is full of flaws and blemishes, it warns you that you will not be appreciated and well received. It warns you to expect pain and loss and hurt in life. When a portrait is attractive, the features strong and confident, the world seems more giving, and ambitions seem more possible.

Many of your core beliefs operate outside of your awareness. While it might be possible for you to identify certain feelings of unworthiness or vulnerability or incompetence, their influence on your daily choices may remain largely invisible. Because so much is at stake, it is crucial that you make your core beliefs conscious, that you examine them as clearly and honestly as you can.

This book will help you to recognize your core beliefs as well as their effect on daily living. The next chapter contains a list of major core beliefs and exercises to help you identify those beliefs that are influencing, for good or bad, your feelings and behavior.

But recognition is only the first step. This book will also help you to *question* your beliefs, to evaluate their accuracy. Some of what you see in your self-portrait is absolutely true. Some of it may be distorted or downright false. Soon you will begin a process of challenging, testing, and evaluating your core beliefs. There is no escaping their influence. But distorted, limiting, and fear-inducing beliefs can be modified. How you see yourself can change. There are ways for Simon to explore and challenge his long-held sense of unworthiness. There are ways for Carmen to test her feelings of incompetence, to begin to see more clearly her strengths as well as weaknesses.

The process of recognizing your beliefs and then challenging and testing them is hard work. But the potential rewards are enormous: a significant change in your sense of worth. An easing of fear. A willingness to take new risks. A sense of freedom.

The Invisible Strings

Core beliefs influence your life in two major ways. First, they establish rules for survival and coping. Second, they set the tone of a constant inner monologue by which you interpret events and evaluate your performance.

The Rules

Once you accept a certain picture of yourself and your relationship to the world, you must, by necessity, establish basic rules for how you will survive. Because Simon considered himself flawed and unworthy, he developed the following strategies for coping with anticipated rejection:

1. Never let anyone really get to know you.
2. Always look good.
3. Always withdraw at the first sign of conflict.
4. Find out what people want and give it to them. If you don't, they will reject you.
5. You must be very, very competent at what you do or you'll be rejected.
6. No one wants to hear the truth about you. Don't share your feelings. Don't let anybody know if you've been hurt.
7. Don't ask for anything. Nobody wants to give it to you.

8. Take care of yourself as best you can. No one else will ever really care about you.

As you can see, Simon's core beliefs engendered specific psychological edicts. Each of these rules had a governing influence on how he conducted himself in relationships. Each of the rules was a logical outcome, a necessary adaptive strategy in a world where he was worthless and those who came to recognize his worthlessness would reject him. For Simon to survive as a "worthless" person, he had to protect himself. He used his rules of living as a behavioral shield to defend himself against the rejection he expects.

Carmen's rules are very different. Her sense of incompetence requires that she:

1. Never make an overt decision.

2. Never directly pursue your needs, because you'll never get them met anyway.

3. Recognize that either you won't get the person you want or he'll turn out to be a bum. So just enjoy whoever comes along and takes an interest in you.

4. Don't try anything new. Either it'll be awful or you'll mess it up.

5. Don't try to take care of yourself. You don't know how to do it and you'll screw it up.

6. It's better to do nothing than to blow it.

Notice that Carmen's rules keep her from taking any risks. They entrench her in a helpless position. She expects to fail and she expects to make the wrong decision, so her rules adaptively require that she change nothing and maintain the status quo.

The rules have an absolute quality. It feels like breaking them would cause some catastrophe. Simon expects that if he reveals his loneliness or fear, people will react with contempt. They'll shun or ridicule him. Carmen assumes that making a career decision will result in some painful and humiliating defeat. Everyone will see how stupid she is.

The price of breaking the rules is to be crushed. Everyone knows that if you jump off a ten-story building, gravity will smash you to the earth. With the same certainty, you've come to expect disaster from any deviation from the strategies formed out of your core beliefs.

The Monologue

Core beliefs affect a second level of your experience. Every minute of your conscious life, you are talking to yourself — interpreting your experience, judging, making assumptions about the feelings and motivations of others, predicting outcomes, trying to figure out what things mean. This is natural. It's how human beings survive. This ability to interpret, look for meanings, attribute causes, and make assumptions is what separates us from lower animals.

But while the monologue is adaptive, helping you to understand your environment, it can also be painful and inhibiting. The inner monologue frequently reflects your core beliefs and rules. It applies them to the particular circumstance in which you now find yourself. For example, when Simon goes out on a first date, he says to himself: "Stop telling her about your mother, stupid. She'll see how screwed up that relationship is." Simon's monologue evaluates his conversation and stops him from taking steps toward intimacy. Carmen's monologue defeats her in a different way. When her boss dumps a pile of extra work on her desk, she says to herself: "So what else can you do? Nothing. You're not going anywhere."

Notice how Simon and Carmen say self-defeating things when faced with challenges that touch on negative core beliefs. The monologue immobilizes them. It makes them afraid to take risks, to try something new. It makes them return to the safe, tried-and-true strategies of coping that also keep them feeling stuck and hopeless.

Putting It Together

The following diagram, developed by Christine Padesky (1989), shows how core beliefs, the rules, and the monologue all work together.

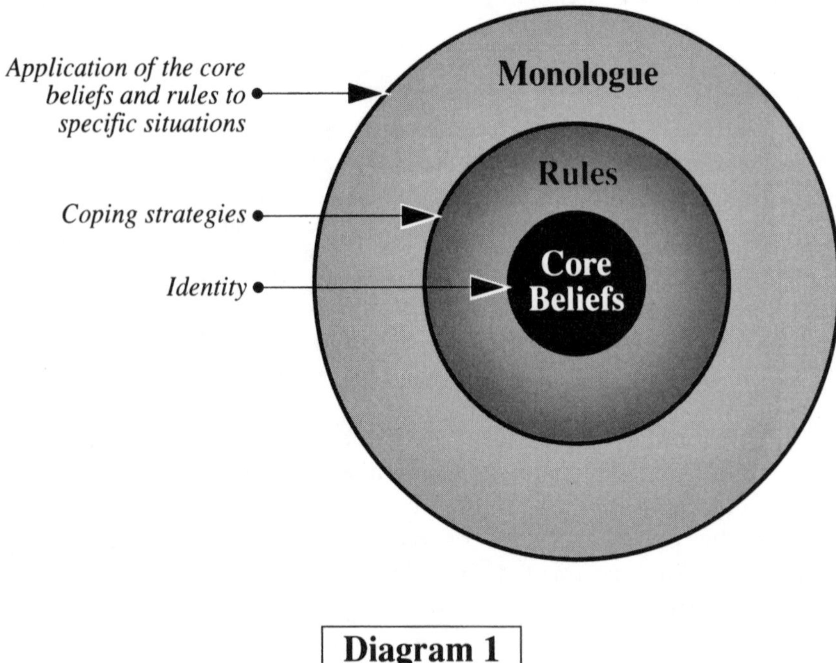

Diagram 1

Consider the case of Rebekah. One of her core beliefs concerns vulnerability. She sees herself as extremely susceptible to harm and illness. She feels inadequate to cope with anything unusual — either feelings inside her body or challenges in the world. Life feels dangerous. The combination of vulnerability and feelings of incompetence has forced Rebekah to make certain rules:

1. Don't go anyplace new. You will feel overwhelmed and panicked if you do.

2. Don't let anybody do you favors. They might expect you to do something different and scary in return.

3. Don't do aerobics. It makes your heart race and gives you that flushed feeling — it's weird and scary.

4. Don't get in a plane. You'll freak out.

5. Don't go downtown. It's too crowded and full of weird people.

6. Don't go out with John. The sexual feelings are too intense, too out of control.

7. Don't get into the Lakeshore Project at work. You'll probably be expected to go to Chicago.

8. Get a new car that won't break down. It's terrifying when old cars break down.

Now notice how Rebekah's core belief of vulnerability and her rule about going downtown affect her monologue when she has to pick up papers from a lawyer on the 35th floor.

> It's full of freaks down here. They ask for spare change, but they'd just as soon knock you on the head and take your purse. I hate this. Too many people. They all look hassled and angry. God, now the elevator. I hate that weightless feeling when it slows down, and the rattling. Thirty-five floors straight down under me. This jerk is going to keep me waiting. I'm going to get stressed out and exhausted just coping with this whole corporate scene down here.

Rebekah's core beliefs are affecting every second of the trip downtown and turning an inconvenience into a nightmare. Her monologue converts her beliefs and rules into situation-specific warnings. Each self-statement triggers adrenalin release, and she experiences an uncomfortable surge of stress hormones. Her tension mounts as she barrages herself with catastrophic thoughts.

Also notice how her expectation of distress becomes a self-fulfilling prophecy: her monologue actually induces the stress response she fears and expects, thus confirming her core belief in her own vulnerability.

How Core Beliefs Are Formed

Core beliefs are by nature *dichotomous*: they inevitably group experiences into positive and negative categories. This grouping is adaptive because it helps you make decisions. You can very quickly conceptualize an event as potentially painful or pleasurable, safe or threatening, good or bad, and something you can or cannot cope with. In doing so, you are making a *prediction* about the outcome. Your core beliefs are like a crystal ball — they help you read the future.

A primitive walking near a cave has a sudden image of the tiger that might be lurking inside. Tigers, he knows, are dangerous, threatening, and too much for an unarmed man. Within seconds, he is running like hell in the other direction. His core belief about vulnerability has allowed him to make a quick, life-preserving decision.

As you grow up, you begin making mental lists of events that are similar in character, outcome, plot, and so on. These events are templates to which you compare new experiences to see if there are any similarities. Your father used to criticize you for being late. Now, when you are late, you expect your boyfriend to do the same thing. These experiences contribute to a core belief about your own vulnerability and competence, and a rule that says "Watch out — men hurt and reject me." Notice how core beliefs allow you to predict outcomes in new situations. This is adaptive for the primitive with the tiger, and it is adaptive for you *when your beliefs are accurate.*

Consider William, who has a core belief about control. He sees himself as incapable of controlling his habits and impulses.

Among other problems, he struggles with binge eating. This core belief that he lacks control helps him make a decision when his sister asks him to prepare a potluck main dish for her retirement party. Within milliseconds, his mind has formed the image of endless snacking while he cooks. That image is connected to the sense of being out of control, memories of bingeing, and feelings of being a bad person. It doesn't take William long to say no to his sister's request. The core belief has helped him make an adaptive decision.

Your core beliefs can also lead you astray. Like Carmen and Simon, you can have inaccurate beliefs about yourself which lead to unrealistic predictions. Simon feels worthless, and in virtually every interpersonal situation, he predicts that he will be rejected if his true reactions and feelings are seen. Carmen feels incompetent and predicts that she will "screw up" any challenge she takes on.

In summary, the formation of core beliefs is an inevitable and adaptive process. It helps you compare current situations with past experience. It helps you predict outcomes and make decisions based on a group of memories that are all categorized by theme.

How Core Beliefs Are Maintained

Once a core belief has been established, there are two natural processes that tend to perpetuate its influence. The first process is called *confirmatory bias* (Meichenbaum 1988). This is your propensity to accept only the information that confirms an existing viewpoint. Everyone tends to ignore data that contradicts established beliefs. It's a kind of filtering, a matter of selective attention. You simply fail to notice or remember events that don't match how you see yourself or the world.

Diagram 2 shows how this happens.

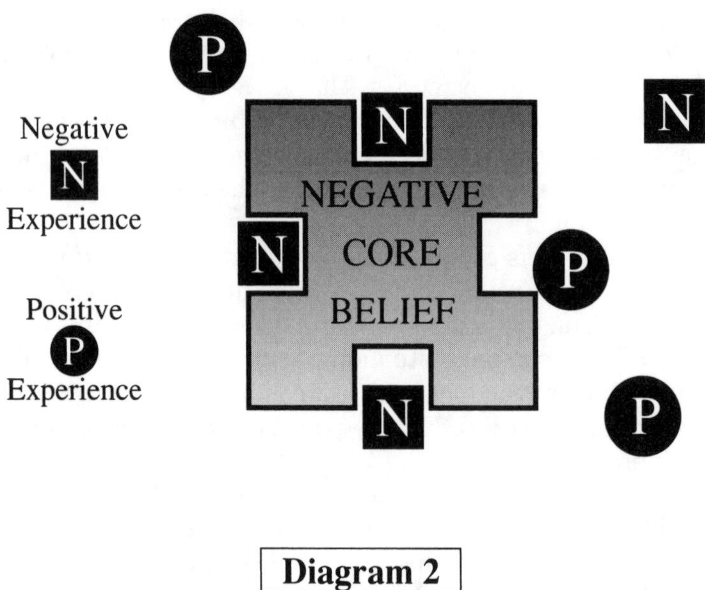

Diagram 2

Notice that positive experiences have the wrong shape to ever be incorporated into the negative core belief. The positive experience doesn't fit, so it is simply ignored. It never gets recorded in memory because you tend to remember things through a process of sorting. You find a place to put recent events — a niche or a category of similar experiences. If no corresponding positive belief matches a positive experience, the experience is usually forgotten.

The opposite situation occurs for optimists who lack core beliefs to categorize or record negative experiences (see Diagram 3). Through confirmatory bias, they remember only the life data that supports existing positive views of the self and world.

You can see how you are likely to get stuck with a belief once it gets formed. The truth is that you *actively* pay attention only to what supports your preset vision of reality. If you have negative core beliefs, you sort through incoming data to selectively attend only to the part of your experience that matches the

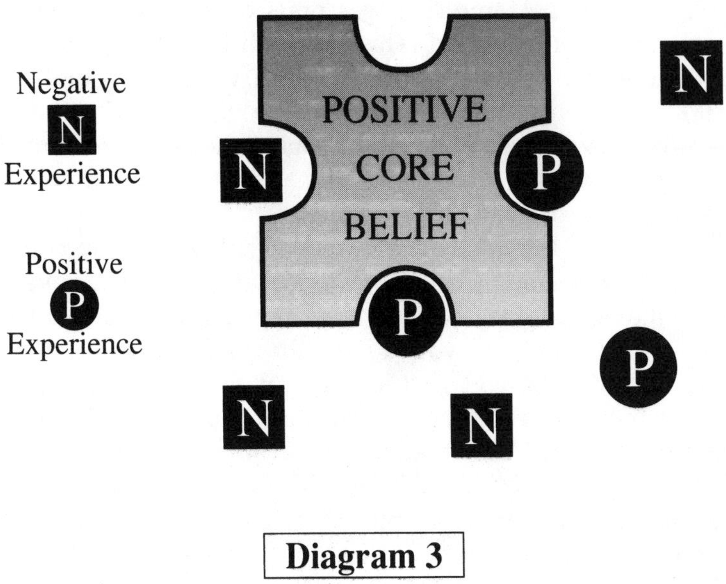

Diagram 3

beliefs. The rest is discounted or ignored. Each core belief has a long list of memories which can be called up at any time and which functions as "proof" for the belief. But sadly you have very little access to all the events of the past that might "prove" some other or even opposite viewpoint.

Consider Simon again. He has too much to drink at the office Christmas party and talks to a young woman about "always feeling like I'm putting on a show, trying to look good. But it's bullshit. I don't feel very good inside, you know?" She is sympathetic and interested, but Simon later dismisses her response as pity and reads the shy smile that she gives him the next day as a confirmation that she is embarrassed and avoiding him.

When a former girlfriend broke up with Simon, she complained that he was cold and remote, that she never felt let in. She knew there was a good person in there somewhere, but he was staving her out by never exposing his feelings. Unfortunately, this feedback didn't fit Simon's negative core beliefs. So he did some cutting and trimming to make it fit. "She finally saw through me," he told himself. "She sees what a cripple I am inside."

Carmen is the same. She was praised at work for developing an organizational chart. This praise didn't fit her core belief of incompetence, so she dismissed her work as "something I should have done a lot sooner." On the other hand, when the sales reports were a day late, she kicked herself for "screwing up the simplest job." Carmen only noticed and remembered what fit her existing frame of reality.

There is a second mechanism that supports your core beliefs. This mechanism is called *mental grooving*. These grooves are the psychological ruts that everyone returns to in situations of stress or uncertainty. If you don't fully understand a situation or you feel anxious, you start looking for some quickly available memory, thought, information, or assumption that will help you decide what to do. Your core beliefs are the preconceptions, the mental grooves, that help you decide how to act in ambiguous situations. When Simon's former girlfriend first brought up her desire to know him better, he began to feel anxious. To help him cope, he quickly fell into the old mental grooves of his core beliefs about his basic flaws and worthlessness. He suspected that she was seeing something she didn't like. Perhaps that something was a glimpse of the emptiness he struggled with. It was time, Simon thought, to get every hair in place and make absolutely sure that nothing leaked out.

Carmen experienced mental grooving when a girlfriend suggested she move out of her grandmother's house and join her as a roommate. The anxiety generated by this new possibility quickly sent Carmen looking for any memories, information, or assumptions that might be relevant to this decision. She remembered burning up a meal she once tried to cook for her father, she recalled her difficulty budgeting, she remembered friends who had withdrawn just at the moment she was counting on them most, she remembered her helpless silence when she felt other relationships slipping away. She experienced a sense of herself as too scattered, too "ungrown-up" to cope. In the process of this mental grooving, Carmen forgot her strengths:

that she was good at keeping a place clean, that her friend often said how much fun she was to talk to, that she had saved over $3,000, that she had traveled to Europe by herself, and that lately she had felt very comfortable and safe with a group of young women at the office. Carmen decided to stay with her grandmother because her core belief of incompetence wouldn't let her see the ways she was growing and learning how to take care of herself.

Coping With Core Beliefs

The remainder of this book will create an opportunity for you to examine, question, and test some of your core beliefs. Some of your core beliefs may be accurate, but some may be inaccurate and maintained only by confirmatory bias and mental grooving. You may find that you have left out big chunks of your history and experience that didn't fit your beliefs.

The goal of this book is not to change your beliefs from one pole to the other, from negative to positive, from black to white. That isn't the way reality works. The goal is to turn some core beliefs that are based on an inaccurate filtering of your life experience in a more realistic direction. You are not expected to give up your beliefs, but just to question them, to put them to the test, to find out if you've had experiences that could make the belief less extreme. Carmen won't be able to move from seeing herself as totally incompetent to seeing herself as fully competent. But if she is able to include all of her life experiences, her core belief will shift so that she can see herself somewhere in the middle of the continuum between hopeless incompetence and unfailing competence. She will not only continue to see areas of weakness, but also begin to see areas of strength. Instead of Simon seeing himself as wholly worthless, he can begin to recognize those times when he has shown more intimate parts of himself and was not rejected.

In this book you will not be bombarded with a set of canned values that you are expected to adopt wholesale. You will be asked instead to become a personal scientist, to investigate your past and your present with as much openness and honesty as you can. You will be asked to experiment, to take risks, and to record the outcomes so that you can realistically test deeply held beliefs about yourself. Only by testing, experimenting, and noticing what happens can you determine the truth of what you have believed for so long.

2

Identifying Your Core Beliefs

You may or may not be aware of your core beliefs right now. Most likely you are in touch with one or two, but the full scope of your beliefs remains unclear.

This chapter will help you identify your core beliefs and bring them sharply into focus. You'll try two different approaches. First, taking the Core Beliefs Inventory will show you how you rate yourself in ten areas of life that often contain troublesome core beliefs. The second approach is the Monologue Diary, where you keep track of your painful feelings, the situations in which they arise, and the inner monologues that typically make you feel bad. By analyzing the situations and your self-statements, you can uncover your underlying core beliefs.

Both approaches are valuable. The Core Beliefs Inventory is relatively simple and easy, providing quick insights and a clear overview of common core beliefs. The Monologue Diary takes more time, but it helps you capture the unique, particular flavor of your core beliefs — the overtones and shadings that can come only from your own experiences.

It's important that you actually *do* the exercises, not just read through the instructions and *imagine* doing them. The exercises are not just a way of imparting information. The experience of doing the exercises will teach you valuable self-examination skills on which your success in using the rest of the book depends.

Core Beliefs Inventory

Adapted in part from Jeffrey Young's (1990) Schema Questionnaire

After each of the 100 statements that follow, circle T or F according to whether you think the statement is mostly true or mostly false. In cases where it's a close decision, go with your first impulse. It's important to complete every item, circling the T or the F (but not both), in order to get an accurate score at the end. But this is not a test — there are no right or wrong answers, or better and worse ways to complete the inventory.

	Mostly True	*Mostly False*	
1.	T	F	I am worthy of love and respect.
2.	T	F	My world is a pretty safe place.
3.	T	F	I perform many tasks well.
4.	T	F	I am in control of my life.
5.	T	F	I feel loved and cared for.
6.	T	F	I can rely upon myself.
7.	T	F	The world is neither fair nor unfair.
8.	T	F	I feel a strong sense of belonging in my family and community.
9.	T	F	Most people can be trusted.
10.	T	F	I set reasonable standards for myself.
11.	T	F	I often feel flawed or defective.
12.	T	F	Life is dangerous — a medical, natural, or financial disaster could strike any time.
13.	T	F	I'm basically incompetent.

14.	T	F	I have very little control over my life.
15.	T	F	I've never felt really cared for by my family.
16.	T	F	Others can care for me better than I can care for myself.
17.	T	F	I get upset when I don't get what I want — I hate to take no for an answer.
18.	T	F	I frequently feel left out of groups.
19.	T	F	Many people would like to hurt me or take advantage of me.
20.	T	F	Very little of what I do satisfies me — I usually think I could do better.
21.	T	F	I feel OK about myself.
22.	T	F	I can protect myself from most dangers.
23.	T	F	Doing some things comes easy for me.
24.	T	F	I have the power I need to solve most of my problems.
25.	T	F	I have at least one satisfying intimate relationship.
26.	T	F	It's OK to disagree with others.
27.	T	F	I accept it when I don't get what I want.
28.	T	F	I fit in well with my circle of friends.
29.	T	F	I rarely need to protect or guard myself with other people.
30.	T	F	I can forgive myself for failure.

31. T F Nobody I desire would desire me if they really got to know me.

32. T F I worry about getting sick or hurt.

33. T F When I trust my own judgment, I make wrong decisions.

34. T F Events just bowl me over sometimes.

35. T F My relationships are shallow — if I disappeared tomorrow, no one would notice.

36. T F I find myself going along with others' plans.

37. T F There are certain things I simply must have to be happy.

38. T F I feel like an outsider.

39. T F Most people think only of themselves.

40. T F I'm a perfectionist; I must be the best at whatever I do.

41. T F I have legitimate needs I deserve to fill.

42. T F I am willing to take risks.

43. T F I am a competent person, as capable as most people.

44. T F My impulses don't control me.

45. T F I feel nurtured in my family.

46. T F I don't need the approval of others for everything I do.

47. T F Things tend to work out, even in the end.

48. T F People usually accept me as I am.

49. T F I seldom feel taken advantage of.

50. T F I set achievable goals for myself.

51. T F I'm dull and boring and can't make interesting conversation.

52. T F If I'm not careful with my money, I might end up with nothing.

53. T F I tend to avoid new challenges.

54. T F I fear I'll give in to overwhelming crying, anger, or sexual impulses.

55. T F I'm afraid of being abandoned — that a loved one will die or reject me.

56. T F I don't function well on my own.

57. T F I feel I shouldn't have to accept some of the limitations placed on ordinary people.

58. T F People don't usually include me in what they're doing.

59. T F Most people can't be trusted.

60. T F Failure is very upsetting to me.

61. T F I count for something in the world.

62. T F I can take care of myself and my loved ones.

63. T F I can learn new skills if I try.

64. T F I can usually control my feelings.

65. T F I can get the care and attention I need.

66. T F I like to spend time by myself.

67.	T	F	Most of the time I feel fairly treated.
68.	T	F	My hopes and dreams are much like everyone else's.
69.	T	F	I give people the benefit of the doubt.
70.	T	F	I'm not perfect and that's OK.
71.	T	F	I'm unattractive.
72.	T	F	I choose my old, familiar ways of doing things over risking the unexpected.
73.	T	F	I don't perform well under stress.
74.	T	F	I'm powerless to change many of the situations I'm in.
75.	T	F	There's no one I can count on for support and advice.
76.	T	F	I try hard to please others, and I put their needs before my own.
77.	T	F	I tend to expect the worst.
78.	T	F	Sometimes I feel like an alien, very different from everybody else.
79.	T	F	I must be on my guard against others' lies and hostile remarks.
80.	T	F	I push myself so hard that I harm my relationships, my health, or my happiness.
81.	T	F	People I like and respect often like and respect me.
82.	T	F	I don't worry much about health or money.

83. T F Most of my decisions are sound.

84. T F I can take charge when I need to.

85. T F I can depend on my friends for advice and emotional support.

86. T F I think for myself, I can stand up for my ideas.

87. T F I'm treated fairly most of the time.

88. T F I could change jobs or join a club and soon fit in.

89. T F I'd rather be too gullible than too suspicious.

90. T F It's OK to make mistakes.

91. T F I don't deserve much attention or respect.

92. T F I feel uneasy when I go very far from home alone.

93. T F I mess up everything I attempt.

94. T F I'm often a victim of circumstances.

95. T F I have no one who hugs me, shares secrets with me, or really cares what happens to me.

96. T F I have trouble making my own wants and needs known.

97. T F Although my life is objectively OK, I have a lot of trouble accepting some parts that aren't the way I'd like them to be.

98. T F I don't feel I belong where I am.

99. T F Most people will break their promises and lie.

100. T F I have very clear, black-and-white rules for myself.

Scoring

This inventory assesses your core beliefs about the ten topics listed below. These topics are important areas of everyone's life, about which everyone has some sort of belief, whether it's conscious or not.

To score your answers, follow these instructions carefully:

1. Value _____ points

Look at your answers for items 1, 21, 41, 61, and 81. For each T circled, give yourself one point.

Now look at your answers for items 11, 31, 51, 71, and 91. For each F circled, give yourself one point.

Record your total points in the space above.

On a scale of one to ten, this indicates how much you agree with the statement "I am worthy." The higher your score, the more valuable you believe you are as a person.

2. Security _____ points

Look at your answers for items 2, 22, 42, 62, and 82. For each T circled, give yourself one point.

Now look at your answers for items 12, 32, 52, 72, and 92. For each F circled, give yourself one point.

Record your total points in the space above.

On a scale of one to ten, this indicates how much you agree with the statement "I am safe." The higher your score, the more safe you feel.

3. Performance _____ points

Look at your answers for items 3, 23, 43, 63, and 83. For each T circled, give yourself one point.

Now look at your answers for items 13, 33, 53, 73, and 93. For each F circled, give yourself one point.

Record your total points in the space above.

On a scale of one to ten, this indicates how much you agree with the statement "I am competent." The higher your score, the more competent you feel.

4. Control _____ points

Look at your answers for items 4, 24, 44, 64, and 84. For each T circled, give yourself one point.

Now look at your answers for items 14, 34, 54, 74, and 94. For each F circled, give yourself one point.

Record your total points in the space above.

On a scale of one to ten, this indicates how much you agree with the statement "I am powerful." The higher your score, the more you feel in control of your life.

5. Love _____ points

Look at your answers for items 5, 25, 45, 65, and 85. For each T circled, give yourself one point.

Now look at your answers for items 15, 35, 55, 75, and 95. For each F circled, give yourself one point.

Record your total points in the space above.

On a scale of one to ten, this indicates how much you agree with the statement "I am loved." The higher your score, the more you feel nurtured.

6. Autonomy _____ points

Look at your answers for items 6, 26, 46, 66, and 86. For each T circled, give yourself one point.

Now look at your answers for items 16, 36, 56, 76, and 96. For each F circled, give yourself one point.

Record your total points in the space above.

On a scale of one to ten, this indicates how much you agree with the statement "I am autonomous." The higher your score, the more independent you feel.

7. Justice _____ points

Look at your answers for items 7, 27, 47, 67, and 87. For each T circled, give yourself one point.

Now look at your answers for items 17, 37, 57, 77, and 97. For each F circled, give yourself one point.

Record your total points in the space above.

On a scale of one to ten, this indicates how much you agree with the statement "I am treated justly." The higher your score, the more likely you are to accept what you get in life as fair or reasonable.

8. Belonging _____ points

Look at your answers for items 8, 28, 48, 68, and 88. For each T circled, give yourself one point.

Now look at your answers for items 18, 38, 58, 78, and 98. For each F circled, give yourself one point.

Record your total score in the space above.

On a scale of one to ten, this indicates how much you agree with the statement "I belong." The higher your score, the more you feel secure and connected to family, friends, acquaintances, and humanity in general.

9. Others _____ points

Look at your answers for items 9, 29, 49, 69, and 89. For each T circled, give yourself one point.

Now look at your answers for items 19, 39, 59, 79, and 99. For each F circled, give yourself one point.

Record your total score in the space above.

On a scale of one to ten, this indicates how much you agree with the statement "People are good." The higher your score, the more likely you are to trust others and to expect them to behave positively towards you.

10. Standards _____ points

Look at your answers for items 10, 30, 50, 70, and 90. For each T circled, give yourself one point.

Now look at your answers for items 20, 40, 60, 80, and 100. For each F circled, give yourself one point.

Record your total points in the space above.

On a scale of one to ten, this indicates how much you agree with the statement "My standards are reasonable and flexible."

The higher your score, the more likely you are to judge your own and others' actions compassionately.

To get a quick overview of your scores, you can fill in the bar chart on the following page. Color in each bar, starting at the bottom, and extending up to your score for that category.

Interpreting Your Scores

It's tempting to visualize the bars on this chart as the bars of a prison. The higher the bars, the more confined and restricted by your beliefs you may feel. The lower the bars, the more freedom and choices you may have in life.

But the Core Belief Inventory is just a guideline. It's designed to help you start to identify your core beliefs, not to pass judgment on them or on yourself. The inventory reveals how you see yourself in the world, based on your experiences. The result isn't good or bad.

[1] Value	[2] Performance	[3] Security	[4] Control	[5] Love	[6] Autonomy	[7] Justice	[8] Belonging	[9] Others	[10] Standards
1	1	1	1	1	1	1	1	1	1
2	2	2	2	2	2	2	2	2	2
3	3	3	3	3	3	3	3	3	3
4	4	4	4	4	4	4	4	4	4
5	5	5	5	5	5	5	5	5	5
6	6	6	6	6	6	6	6	6	6
7	7	7	7	7	7	7	7	7	7
8	8	8	8	8	8	8	8	8	8
9	9	9	9	9	9	9	9	9	9
10	10	10	10	10	10	10	10	10	10

People who score high in agreement with the ten basic belief statements may tend to have a greater sense of well-being than those who score low. But right now that isn't the point. What matters is getting an honest sense of what you have come to believe about yourself.

So take this inventory with several grains of salt. Use it to find out where you stand on these core questions, but don't beat yourself up about your results. You believe what you believe. It is literally true for you at this moment, and you can't just decide to believe something else because it will give you a "better" score.

Likewise, don't get stuck in the idea that there are exactly ten possible core beliefs. Ten is just a convenient number. It makes the inventory work neatly. But you could make a strong case for love and belonging being such similar issues that they're part of the same belief. Or you could say that safety and the good or evil nature of others are part of the same belief about how vulnerable you are. And we have undoubtedly left out some belief that is very important to you. For example, in planning this book, we chose early on not to cover beliefs about the existence of God, spirituality, the afterlife, and so on.

The diary techniques that follow will help you refine your core belief statements and explore some that the inventory may not have elicited.

Monologue Diary

In a way, this exercise "sneaks up" on core beliefs by starting with something that is more self-evident: your feelings in a given situation.

Do this exercise for at least a week. During that week, pay special attention to any painful emotions such as as anxiety, guilt, depression, embarrassment, or anger. As soon as possible after you notice a painful emotion, write down the feeling, the situation, and what you were saying to yourself in your internal monologue just before you felt bad. Use the three-column format shown below.

Feeling	*Situation*	*Monologue*

Here's an example of a diary completed by Lilly, a medical transcriptionist, during the first month of night school, where she was studying accounting and bookkeeping. She hoped to get a better job doing bookkeeping and eventually get a degree in business administration.

Feeling	*Situation*	*Monologue*
Nervous, scared	Waiting for teacher to pass out first quiz	"I can't do this."
Depressed	Reading assignment	"Dense"
Sad, let down, irritated	Talking to Sherri on the phone about job possibilities	(Just an image of her smiling and shaking her head the way she does.)
Discouraged, hopeless	Getting a "C" on the first quiz	"I barely passed the easy part. I'll never finish this. It's hopeless."
Furious	When John said I was wasting my time	"He doesn't care about me."
Anxious, agitated	Trying to get out of work on time and get to class	"Late...flunk...awful."
Sad, crying	Trying to complete balance sheet problems at two a.m.	"I'm nothing, never will be anything."

Anxious	Waiting to ask the financial aid people if I qualify	(Rehearsing my lines, seeing them smile sadly and shake their heads.)

Notice how Lilly had trouble identifying some of her monologues. Sometimes she could only remember a single word or a mental image. This is very common. If this happens to you, you can expand on what you remember by using your imagination.

To use your imagination to remember monologues, lie down in a quiet place where you won't be disturbed for five minutes. Close your eyes and take some deep breaths. Try to consciously relax every muscle in your body and put your cares aside for this moment. In your mind's eye, see yourself reliving the particular situation from your diary. See the situation as if it were a movie, but run it in slow motion. Imagine that an announcer is doing a "voice-over" commentary on the action, providing you with the missing monologue.

For example, before going to sleep one night, Lilly visualized herself preparing for her visit to the financial aid office. She saw herself waiting in the hall, getting up nerve to go in. She slowed the scene down by concentrating on the fine details: the two-toned green institutional paint, the smell of dust and disinfectant, the flickering fluorescent lights, the hum of classes going on behind closed doors. As she saw the scene in her mind, she heard her own voice whispering: "They'll smile and be nice, but they'll say no. They really think I'm just a silly woman. Just silly Lilly, like my Dad always said. Off on another harebrained scheme. This will never work. Why should they help me?"

Lilly also used visualization to relive the scene with her friend on the telephone. She found that her mental image of her friend's face translated into these thoughts: "She thinks I'm chasing rainbows again. She's just too nice to say so. She senses my self-doubt and secretly agrees that I'll never get a better job." And the slow motion version of "Late...flunk...awful" was a predictable "I'm going to be late. The teacher will think I don't care and flunk me out. This is awful. I can't stand it."

Work on your own diary entries until you have a big crop of feelings, situations, and monologues. The more you practice this exercise, the better you will get at tuning into your monologues and seeing how they can cause those painful feelings that previously seemed to "flare up" out of nowhere.

It's exciting to learn how to uncover your monologues, but even more fascinating is what you can do with the material from your diary once you have at least a week's worth of material to work with. The next two exercises will show you how to discover your core beliefs by analyzing your negative monologues and the situations in which they typically occur.

Laddering

Laddering is a way of analyzing your monologue statements, looking for more and more basic underlying assumptions and predictions, until you arrive at statements of core belief. The technique is called laddering because it proceeds step by step, like descending a ladder rung by rung.

Laddering has only two rules. Rule one is to question yourself by using this format: "What if ________________? What does that mean to me?" In the blank space, you write a self-statement from your internal monologue. Then you write the answer to the question "What does that mean to me?" Next, you start over, using your answer to fill in the blank. Here's how Lilly did it with one of her monologues:

I barely passed the easy part.

What if I barely passed the easy part? What does that mean to me?

It means when the material gets harder I'll flunk out.

What if I flunk out? What does that mean to me?

It means I won't get my degree.

What if I don't get my degree, what does that mean to me?

It means I can't improve myself, I'm stuck being a glorified typist.

What if I'm stuck being a typist? What does that mean to me?
It means I'll stay poor.
What if I stay poor? What does that mean to me?
It means I'm not competent.
What if I'm incompetent? What does that mean to me?
It means just that — I'm incompetent to do what I want to do.

At this point, Lilly could go no further. Whenever she asked herself what being incompetent meant, she just thought it was self-evident. It was the basic statement beneath her unhappiness: that she was just not competent to do the things she wanted to do.

Here's another example of Lilly's laddering:

He doesn't care about me.
What if he doesn't care about me? What does that mean to me?
It means I'm not very important.
What if I'm not very important? What does that mean to me?
It means I have no value.
What if I have no value. What does that mean to me?
It means I'm worthless.
What if I'm worthless? What does that mean to me?
It means I have no worth.

In this case, Lilly "hit bottom" quickly. The horrible judgment "I'm worthless" summed up everything that lay beneath her feelings of not being cared for by people: she wasn't cared for because she wasn't worth anyone's care.

When you try laddering, look out for rule number two: don't answer with a feeling. It's common to resort to feelings instead of self-statements in this exercise. For example, "What does being poor mean to me?" might be answered "I'll be miserably unhappy." But that kind of feeling statement leads nowhere. Keep your answers confined to statements that express conclusions or beliefs or assumptions...not descriptions of feelings.

Theme Analysis

This is another way to use your diary material to uncover core beliefs. It involves looking not at the monologues but at the situations themselves. You analyze the situations, looking for common themes that connect them.

Rudy was a pastry chef who was keeping his diary to try to figure out why he felt so guilty and inadequate in his relationship with his girlfriend, Gloria. Here are the situations he listed in his diary:

Coming home later than I said I would
Forgetting our six months' anniversary
When Gloria asked me not to be so rough in lovemaking
Buying her the ring that was too large
Discussing where to go over Labor Day
The flat tire on the way to her mother's house
Making a tactless remark about her best friend
Too much almond paste in her birthday cake

Looking at just the situations, Rudy saw a theme emerging: he couldn't bear to make mistakes around Gloria. Any deviation from perfection destroyed his image of himself as the perfect lover and companion, and somehow stole his enjoyment of their time together. He realized that he had very rigid standards about how to love someone.

Linda was a physical therapist who remained depressed even though she had a well-paying job, good health, and a stable relationship. Looking at the situations she found depressing was very informative:

The annual evaluation at work, even though it was positive
Receiving birthday presents
A friend being diagnosed as having breast cancer
Looking into the mirror and deciding I look weird
Having to ask my boss for a favor
Being asked to present in-service training at the hospital

Having to be stern with patients who haven't done their exercises
My husband saying "I love you"
A disagreement over scheduling at work
Discussing a move to a newer, nicer apartment

At first, these situations seemed to have little in common. Some were at work, some were at home, some were by herself, some were with others. She felt she was "crazy" because events that would make most people happy frequently made her feel sad, out of place, an undeserving impostor.

The sense of being an impostor, of being undeserving, finally showed Linda the common theme: all the problem situations were ones in which attention was focused on her. In each case, she was being judged or compared or honored or criticized. Even birthday presents and declarations of love were painful because she didn't feel she deserved them. At her core, she didn't believe that she was worthy of any attention, any honor, any love. Her core belief that robbed normally happy experiences of all pleasure was a belief in her own worthlessness.

Theme analysis can also be done directly on your monologue statements. For instance, this is a summary of Hilary's typical internal monologue while at work running her restaurant:

> There goes Tony, sneaking out back again. Probably smoking dope back by the trash bins. Got to keep an eye on him... That guy at table six looks shifty and nervous. Bet he tries to beat the check...Running late, got to find time to inventory the meat locker. Is the chef in cahoots with the butcher? Must be over-ordering and grabbing kickbacks, cheating me... Marcy should have been back from her break by now. She's so lazy.

Laddering down isn't necessary here. The theme emerges readily as you spot key words: *sneaking...keep an eye on...shifty, beat the check...in cahoots...kickbacks...cheating...lazy.* Hilary obviously believes that other people are not to be trusted, that they are out to cheat her, and that she must be constantly vigilant or else she'll be taken advantage of.

When you have identified your major core beliefs, you'll be ready for the next step — analyzing the consequences of your beliefs. In the next chapter, you'll explore both the positive and negative effects your beliefs have on your mood, your relationships, your work, and every other area of your life.

3

Consequences of Core Beliefs

Your core beliefs have far-reaching consequences, both positive and negative, in every area of your life. Core beliefs affect your mood, your relationships, your job, what you do for fun, and even your physical health.

It's easy to see how certain core beliefs can affect your mood negatively. For example, if you hold the belief that the universe is a hostile place full of danger, your mood will be colored by anxiety, as you constantly brace yourself against calamities. On the other hand, if you consider the world a relatively safe place, your prevailing mood will be calmer and more relaxed.

Core beliefs tend to reinforce each other, making their effect on your mood even more profound. A case in point is the MacMillan sisters. June MacMillan is known in her family as a "Pollyanna" because she is so cheerful all the time, while her sister Nelly is called "grumpy Nell." Cheerful June believes that she is loved, that she is treated fairly most of the time, and that she really belongs in her family group and community. Grumpy Nell holds the opposite beliefs: that few people really care for her, that she usually gets the "dirty end of the stick," and that she doesn't really fit in with her friends and neighbors, with whom she quarrels frequently. The sisters' upbringing, life experiences, and current circumstances are very similar. The crucial difference is one of belief. June's positive convictions make her world an open, sunny field, whereas Nell's negative beliefs make her world a dark prison.

Relationships

The consequences of core beliefs show up most vividly in relationships. Your core beliefs can literally make or break a love affair, a marriage, or a family.

If you have extremely high standards for yourself and others, you may never find someone who measures up to your ideal. Or if you have a basic doubt that there is enough love and nurturance available for you in the world, you may take anyone who comes along or give up looking for a partner entirely. You might also miss out on love just because you don't believe you're worthy of it.

However, if you have reasonable standards and believe that you are worthy of love and that there are numerous appropriate partners out there for you, your chances of finding someone are increased enormously.

Core beliefs have the biggest effects in intimate relationships. For instance, Jack and Susie had been married for two years when he took a job that required him to be away from home three days a week. Up to that point, Susie's lack of belief in her own autonomy and her dependence on Jack had not been a problem. But now she was on her own half the time. She suddenly had to deal with the landlord, with her car breaking down, with finding things to do in the evenings, and worst of all, with horrible feelings of being alone, exposed, and vulnerable. After several tearful phone conversations and all-night arguments, Jack agreed to give up the job. But he was very resentful, and this conflict was the beginning of the end of their marriage.

Core beliefs affect your sex life as well. For example, Peter and Sarah finally broke up, largely because their sexual contact was unsatisfactory. It seemed that Peter wanted her to initiate sex more often, while Sarah wanted him to sweep her off her feet more often and stop asking "Did you come?" when it was all over. It turned out that they shared incompatible core beliefs. Sarah believed that she had little control over her life, including their sexual life together. She didn't feel powerful enough to seize control of the situation and initiate sex. Peter had a similar feeling of powerlessness that prevented him from being the dynamic lover that Sarah fantasized about. Plus, his high, rigid standards would allow him to make love in only one way, with an invariable tempo and sequence of actions that had to culminate in simultaneous orgasm or else the whole enterprise was a failure.

The number and quality of your friendships are affected by your core beliefs as well. If you believe that other people are basically good, trustworthy, and interesting, you'll tend to make friends easily. Strangers will sense your attitude and find you good, trustworthy, and interesting as well. If you also believe in reasonable standards for your own and others' behavior, you'll have an easier time keeping friends through the inevitable conflicts that arise. But if you automatically distrust strangers on principle, and compare their behavior to a rigid standard, you'll have fewer and shorter friendships.

If you have children, your core beliefs will determine the quality of your parenting and the beliefs that your children develop. For example, Marianne had deep doubts about her competence as a mother. She would often set up rules and later change her mind and alter the rules. One day she would be strict and stern, the next she'd try the "hands off" approach. Her hesitancy and lack of consistency were picked up by her daughter Janet, who grew up a confused, hesitant adolescent. Janet wondered about her own competence in knowing what the limits were and how to stay within them.

Work

Everything about work is affected by your core beliefs, starting with your choice of career. If you are confident of your abilities and your worth, you will pick a field that really interests you and will stand a good chance of finding rewarding work in your chosen area. But if you come out of high school or college or a divorce plagued by doubts about your competence, you will be more likely to look for something safe and easy, and possibly miss out on a challenging but more rewarding path.

Once you're in a work situation, your performance will be greatly affected by core beliefs such as "I am competent," "I am powerful," or "I am safe." With beliefs like these, you can undertake challenging projects with confidence and stay focused on the task at hand. But if you believe "I am a screw-up" or "I have no control over my job," you will proceed hesitantly, fearing mistakes, criticism, and failure.

A case in point is a pair of social workers named Jacob and Harriet. They worked for the same social services agency, with the same population of clients and many of the same duties. One duty they both shared was attempting to find jobs for handicapped clients. They both had the same list of phone numbers of local businesses that often employed the handicapped, but Harriet placed twice as many clients as Jacob. The big difference was in their core beliefs.

Harriet felt pretty competent and believed she could take control of a situation. Here's Harriet making a placement call:

> Hi, this is Harriet over at Social Services. Listen, I have a terrific woman who's ready to take on a real job. I think you'll love her. Her name's Janie and she lives right in your neighborhood. She's cheerful, prompt, and a hard worker. She'd be just right for putting together those little plastic things you guys make. I could bring her over tomorrow afternoon for an interview.

Jacob, on the other hand, felt incompetent and at the mercy of the bureaucracy. When he finally forced himself to make a placement call, he'd sound like this:

> Hello, this is Jacob Meyer at Social Services. I was wondering if you might have an opening for one of our clients. She has a learning disability and can't read or write, but we think she might be ready for job placement in a sheltered environment that requires limited manual dexterity.

No wonder Harriet outscored him two to one.

When it comes to being creative or taking risks in a job, core beliefs can make a big difference. For example, a high school shop teacher in the Midwest wanted to find an exciting project for his senior students. He was tired of the traditional solutions — drop-leaf tables for wood shop, barbecue grills for metal shop, and hot rods for auto shop. He came up with a plan to combine all three classes and build a kit airplane with wooden wings, a metal fuselage, and a converted auto engine. The school authorities went wild when he proposed this. There was no money, no precedent, no way to change class schedules, no insurance coverage, and no end of other reasons why he couldn't be allowed to build an airplane. But one by one, John figured out creative solutions. His plan required donations from airplane parts suppliers, commitments from students to work after school hours, insurance waivers, favorable publicity in the local papers, and so on. The daring and creativity to pull off a project like this comes from a deeply held core belief in your own autonomy and power. Without that belief in yourself, you can't summon the independence of thought, will, and action it takes.

Play

Recreation or leisure time serves two important and seemingly contradictory purposes. It allows you to relax, and it provides excitement.

Joelle was a forty-year-old seamstress who still lived with her mother. She was very dependent on her mother and felt worthless unless she was "making a contribution." That meant that she spent all her time either sewing customers' drapes and cushions, doing the housework, or taking care of her hypochondriac mother. She didn't feel she deserved any rest or relaxation. She was tired all the time but refused to take a break.

Tim was a U.S. Customs Service clerk who yearned to drive his motorhome up the AlCan highway to visit an army buddy in Anchorage. But he never did. Year after year he spent his vacation driving out to visit his wife's relatives in North Carolina. The core belief that prevented him from embarking on his Alaskan adventure was "It's too risky." He was afraid of breaking down in the middle of nowhere and suffering a heart attack. So he endured the in-laws, humidity, and mosquitoes of August in North Carolina, where he finally died of a heart attack two miles from a hospital.

Health

Some core beliefs are bad for your health. Jim Henson, the creator of the Muppet characters, was a good example. A brilliant but shy and retiring man, he died of a massive infection that could have been easily treated if he had just gone to the doctor. But he hated to bother anybody. He lacked the belief in his own worth and autonomy that would have allowed him to take care of himself, to take his own well-being seriously enough.

At the other extreme, a belief that the world is a dangerous, disease-infested place can lead to full-fledged hypochondria. Or if you believe you can't depend on yourself, you may come to depend on alcohol or drugs and damage your health that way.

On the positive side, you will tend to take good care of yourself if you believe you are worthy, loved and cared for, and in control of your life.

Facing the Consequences Exercise

In this exercise, you will explore the consequences of particular core beliefs in detail. In the space at the top of the form, write one of the core belief statements that you uncovered in the last chapter. Pick a belief that you suspect causes you a lot of trouble, one that you are interested in researching to see if it's accurate. Write out the belief in as much detail as you need to fix it firmly in your mind. Your statement can be a single phrase, a full sentence, or a whole paragraph.

For the belief you've chosen to work on, list all the positive and negative consequences you can think of, considering each of the major areas of your life.

The goal of this exercise is threefold. First, it will help you get a clearer picture of what various beliefs are costing you in terms of negative consequences. The beliefs that are costing you the most are prime candidates for further exploration in later chapters.

The second goal of this exercise is to see how core beliefs may also have positive consequences in your life. You may discover that a belief that is negative in one area of your life is actually helping you in another. You may even decide that there is a net gain — that the costs are outweighed by the benefits.

The third goal of this exercise is to give you practice in seeing how your core beliefs influence and guide you in all areas of your life. This practice will come in handy in a later chapter when you start figuring out how you have expressed your core beliefs as a set of rules that guide your behavior.

Consequences Chart

Core Belief: ____

	Negative Consequences	*Positive Consequences*
MOOD (Your habitual, prevailing feelings that color your existence)		
RELATIONSHIPS (With your spouse or sexual partner, parents, siblings, children, in-laws, friends, strangers)		
WORK (Career choice, performance, risk taking, creativity, relationships with co-workers, job stability and satisfaction)		

	Negative Consequences	*Positive Consequences*
PLAY (Ability to relax, experience pleasure, seek adventure, express yourself creatively, pursue hobbies and interests)		
HEALTH		
OTHER: ________ (Church or volunteer work, political action, and so on)		

Do this exercise for at least three core beliefs and spend some time on each one. The process may be slow at first, but if you persevere, you'll soon get the hang of it and may even need extra sheets of paper to have room for all the details.

To help you see how to fill out this chart, here is one done by Randi, a 35-year-old nurse practitioner and mother of a 3-year-old boy.

Consequences Chart

Core Belief: Other people are basically selfish, greedy, ruthless.

	Negative Consequences	*Positive Consequences*
MOOD (Your habitual, prevailing feelings that color your existence)	Cynical, somewhat depressed.	
RELATIONSHIPS (With your spouse or sexual partner, parents, siblings, children, in-laws, friends, strangers)	Few friends. Distrust even my husband, who loves me. Don't know any of my neighbors. My son has few friends, too. Sex is always a negotiation — can't just let myself go.	I feel protected by my distrust. It's like a suit of armor. Seldom taken by surprise by what others do.
WORK (Career choice, performance, risk taking, creativity, relationships with co-workers, job stability and satisfaction)	My patients don't warm up to me much. I'm more a technician than healer. If I trusted people more, I might have joined the practice that became the best in the county.	Good at collecting bills. Get a lot of work done because I'm not wasting time on gossip and aimless chatter. I drive a hard bargain.

	Negative Consequences	*Positive Consequences*
PLAY (Ability to relax, experience pleasure, seek adventure, express yourself creatively, pursue hobbies and interests)	Have trouble joining group activities. Vacation in Mexico ruined by constant suspicions of being cheated and laughed at. Hard to relax around strangers and have a good time at parties.	I enjoy reading, snorkeling — things I can do by myself.
HEALTH	Headaches, stomach problems.	I always get a second opinion.
OTHER:_______ (Church or volunteer work, political action, and so on)	I don't participate in organized activities. Can't decide if that's positive or negative.	

In Randi's case, her negative beliefs about others cost her a lot while contributing only a little security to her life. That doesn't mean that changing how she related to people was easy or automatic. Although she decided that the cost of not trusting people was too high, she still believed it was best to be very cautious. Don't expect that insights about the consequences of your beliefs will be all it takes to change them.

This next chart was completed by Jack, a mortgage broker who wanted to explore his anxiety over travel.

Consequences Chart

Core Belief: I'm not safe. Life is full of dangers.

	Negative Consequences	*Positive Consequences*
MOOD (Your habitual, prevailing feelings that color your existence)	Anxious if I have to fly in an airplane, travel alone, leave the country, stay in a hotel above the tenth floor.	I feel fine in my own home and neighborhood.
RELATIONSHIPS (With your spouse or sexual partner, parents, siblings, children, in-laws, friends, strangers)	Rarely visit my brother.	My wife hates travel too, likes being safe at home.
WORK (Career choice, performance, risk-taking, creativity, relationships with co-workers, job stability and satisfaction)	No problem.	I'm a natural at spotting unsafe houses and risky loans.
PLAY (Ability to relax, experience pleasure, seek adventure, express yourself creatively, pursue hobbies and interests)	I'll never take up skydiving or mountain climbing.	I like collecting old toys — a nice, safe hobby.
HEALTH	Worry about getting sick.	I make sure I get a checkup every year.

	Negative Consequences	*Positive Consequences*
OTHER: ________ (Church or volunteer work, political action, and so on)		

This is a case in which the negative consequences are very real, but not very confining. Jack was not required by his job, his family, or his aspirations to do any of the things he most feared, such as taking long plane trips out of the country. He could stay safely at home and function quite well while avoiding activities that he considered dangerous. He decided that his core belief about security, whether accurate or not, was not restricting him enough to bother testing it.

Here's another chart, filled out by Heather, an artist who lived with her artist husband, Ray, in a loft in San Francisco and helped make ends meet by cleaning houses.

Consequences Chart

Core Belief: I'm completely dependent on Ray. Without him I can do nothing.

	Negative Consequences	*Positive Consequences*
MOOD (Your habitual, prevailing feelings that color your existence)	Depressed. Anxious when he's gone. Resentful. Hate myself for being such a mouse.	Secure and content when he's around.
RELATIONSHIPS (With your spouse or sexual partner, parents, siblings, children, in-laws, friends, strangers)	My only friends are Ray's friends. My mom bugs me to leave him. When he's mad at me, I get scared and jittery When he doesn't seem to want me sexually, I resent it, but don't say anything or try to start anything myself. I'm terrified he'll leave me.	When he's here and paying attention to me, it's wonderful. And several of Ray's friends are genuinely fond of me for myself.
WORK (Career choice, performance, risk-taking, creativity, relationships with co-workers, job stability and satisfaction)	I compare my painting to his too much. I sacrifice my time for art to take care of his business.	He has taught me a lot. Ray encourages me to finish paintings I might just give up on.

	Negative Consequences	*Positive Consequences*
	I don't know how to create anything that's 100 percent me.	
	Ray's good opinion of my art is so important to me, I'm like a puppy waiting for praise.	
	Cleaning houses is so boring. I'm sure I must be good at something more interesting, but I can't get motivated.	
PLAY (Ability to relax, experience pleasure, seek adventure, express yourself creatively, pursue hobbies and interests)	We only do what Ray wants to do.	We give great parties together.
	I can't relax when he's gone.	
	I'd like to go to Italy, but Ray hates travel.	
HEALTH	I don't take care of myself — had that cyst for weeks before I finally did something about it.	
OTHER: ________ (Church or volunteer work, political action, and so on)	I'd like to do volunteer work for an ecology group, but Ray thinks it's a waste of time, so I never get around to it.	
	How did I get this way?	

Heather is trapped in an unsatisfying life by an unfortunate core belief. Her dependence has her in a velvet trap — confining and stifling, but also familiar and comforting.

Heather's final question is one that you may well be asking yourself. How did you come to believe what you do, and why is it so hard to alter core beliefs? The next chapter takes a look at your core beliefs from an historical perspective and begins to answer this question.

4

Evidence From Your Past

Your core beliefs were formed primarily by experiences from your childhood—some that you consciously remember, some that you don't. As you know, core beliefs create a framework for memory. You tend to remember events that support your core beliefs and forget experiences that don't fit or contradict your deep convictions. So memories tend to constellate around certain key concepts about yourself—your competence, lovability, safety, and so on. And a reciprocal relationship forms between past events and core beliefs—critical events help create core beliefs, but these same beliefs later influence exactly how and what you remember of your past.

One very important thing you can do right now is to take a careful look at your past. Do the experiences you remember really support and verify your core beliefs? You have come to assume that your deep convictions about yourself and the world are true. But you will now have the opportunity to examine your life history with deliberation and care, searching for events that challenge as well as support your beliefs. And, going even further, you can look beneath the surface events to see the circumstances and mitigating conditions that influenced your behavior and experience in the past.

This process of self-examination, first conceived by Jeffrey Young (1984), is called the *Historical Test*. It is a structured way of exploring your childhood to (1) uncover as many memories as possible that either tend to support or contradict a particular core belief, and (2) identify the actual (as opposed to imagined or assumed) causes for each event that lends support to your core belief.

The Historical Test

The first step in the Historical Test is to choose one of the core beliefs that you identified in chapter 2. There's no point in testing beliefs that are positive or at least doing you no apparent harm. Choose one for which you have found significant negative consequences. On top of a piece of 8½- by 11-inch paper, write down a succinct description of your core belief.

Directly underneath your core belief, write "Age 0–3." This is the first era of your life that you will intensively examine regarding the truth or falseness of your belief. Later, on separate sheets of paper, you will examine the age periods 4–6, 7–10, 11–15, and 16–20. But right now you're going to look at your very earliest memories.

To finish setting up your Historical Test, run a line down the middle of the page, making two columns. Over the left-hand column write "Evidence True," and over the right-hand column write "Evidence False." Now set some time aside to immerse yourself in the past. Try to remember everything you can about the first three years of your life that would seem to have any bearing on your core belief. Include not only memories, but also things you have been told about yourself, family jokes and stories about your infancy or early childhood, even tag lines and labels (Jimmy, the cry baby; the dunce; Julie, the princess; the sad sack; and so on). If at all possible, try to trace these labels and tag lines back to specific events or behaviors.

Just do the best you can. It's a long time ago and much of this period of your life will be very hazy. As memories and stories from your past come up, try to determine whether they provide evidence for or against the core belief. If the memory seems irrelevant, don't put it down. If it's relevant to your belief, but you can't decide if it is evidence for or against, make your best guess and temporarily put it in one of the columns.

If you're like most people, you'll initially find many more memories that support your core belief. That's fine. Go ahead and put everything down that seems in any way to suggest that your core belief is true. But it's also important to look for any balancing memories, stories, labels, and tag lines. For example, you might have been told that you cried a lot as an infant. But at the same time, you've been told that you were always content sitting on someone's lap or were easily jollied. If you are looking at a core belief surrounding worth and value, it is important that you include both these pieces of information in your historical test. So go ahead and really search your memory bank for anything that might fit in the Evidence False column for your core belief during this first era of 0–3.

Arlene followed these directions and initially developed the following lists.

I'm Not Very Lovable

Ages 0–3

Evidence True	*Evidence False*
Grandma said I cried a lot.	Sal and I were real good friends.
Colicky.	Mom visited and brought me presents.
Had a real temper when I didn't get my way.	
Mom gave me to Grandma because she couldn't handle me.	
Wet the bed. Upset Grandma.	
Very sick and allergic—real pain in the ass. Always in bed with something.	
Got lost and had to be brought home by a policeman. Grandma angry.	
Hit another little girl with a band-aid box when she tried to take it. Needed stitches.	
Grandma complained I watched too much TV.	

Arlene realized as she looked at the list that she hadn't fully explored memories that somehow made her feel lovable.

With some effort, she added the following memories to her Evidence False list:

> Grandma and I sang songs together and she looked happy.
>
> Spent time with Mom, and Grandma said she missed me. Cried when I came back.
>
> Grandma rocking me and hugging me when I couldn't breathe at night.
>
> Grandma once said she loved me more than her own children.
>
> When I moved to Grandma's house, she walked with me around the neighborhood, hand-in-hand, and showed me everything and said, "This is your home now." (I feel tearful remembering this.)

Challenging the Evidence

Once you've identified memories that seem to support your core belief (in the Evidence True column), it's time to carefully evaluate the data you've collected. For each memory that supports your core belief, ask the following five questions:

1. *Was this normal behavior for that age level?* If you're not sure, ask other people. You might even consider reading a book on child development. If it seems very possible that your behavior was normal and age-appropriate, write *normal* next to the item on your list.

2. *Did I have a choice, or was my behavior determined?* Were circumstances such that you literally had to do what you did? Remember, you were a child, and what happened in your world was largely determined by the adults who took care of you. If it feels like you had little choice about your behavior, write *no choice* next to the item.

3. *Was my behavior adaptive? Did it help me cope with difficult circumstances? Was it how I survived?* If it feels like your behavior was a way of adapting to difficult or painful circumstances, write *coping* next to the item.

4. *Is there another explanation for this event besides my core belief?* How would you explain what happened to you if it happened to someone else? Really think about this one. Get some other opinions, some objective input. If you are able to develop an alternative explanation, write it next to the item, or at the bottom of the list.

5. *How might the behavior or event be seen as a positive?* Is there some aspect of this memory that underscores your strengths (for example, your ability to survive) or certain eventual positive outcomes? If you can find a positive side to this memory, you might consider moving it to the other column, or at least adding the positive component to the Evidence False list.

Arlene used the five questions to evaluate the memories that supported the core belief that she was not lovable. She decided that crying a lot and being colicky were normal for the first six months of life. Likewise, having a temper was normal. In addition, having a temper indicated strength and a willingness to push through obstacles. Wetting the bed was also normal, she realized, and is a very typical response to trauma. The more she thought about it, the clearer it seemed that the enuresis had started just after moving to her grandmother's house and leaving her mother. For the allergies and getting lost, Arlene wrote *no choice*. Throwing the Band-Aid box, she remembered, had nothing to do with being a bad, unlovable kid. As she thought back to that time, she realized the real explanation was that she was angry and frightened at the prospect of losing her mother and had no other way of expressing her feelings. The TV watching was clearly adaptive, since it helped her to numb herself during the first scary days at Grandma's house.

You'll notice that as Arlene evaluated her list, most of the memories were converted into normal, adaptive, or necessary acts. Arlene began to see some of her childhood experiences in a different light. She was not unlovable. She was a little girl coping with loss and frightening changes. She was doing the best she could.

Age-Level Summary

At the end of each era, you should write a one paragraph summary of the evidence regarding your core belief. Arlene wrote the following summary for ages 0–3:

> My grandmother seemed to love me, my mother continued to visit, I had a good friend. I was real scared about losing my mother. My temper, the bedwetting, and the TV watching all seem like reactions to that fear. I handled things the best I could for a little girl of three.

Continuing the Historical Test

Now you should continue, using exactly the same process described in the 0–3 age level, with the four succeeding age levels. As you did before, divide the page in half and write memories that support your core belief under the Evidence True column. Memories that might contradict your core belief should appear under Evidence False. With each age level, work toward balance by actively looking for memories that might, in some way, contradict your core belief. Evaluate each item in the Evidence True column with your five questions. Then finish up by writing a summary of the evidence for that particular era.

Here is the rest of Arlene's Historical Test.

Ages 4-6

Evidence True	*Evidence False*
Mom had me for the summer, then sent me back to Grandma. *She was in incredible pain and couldn't really take care of me.*	Sal and I stayed friends, even though I couldn't go over there.

Bedwetting.
Normal.

Lost my coats all the time.
Normal.

Grandma screamed at me for daydreaming and not listening when she told me something.
Coping: I kept it together by having this very active fantasy life.

I was always knocking things down in kindergarten, blocks and stuff. The teacher was mad at me.
Coping: I had all this anger and that's how I dealt with it.

Sal's mother wouldn't let me come over to his house because I broke his record player and I played too rough.
Coping by using my anger.

Mom took me to restaurants and got mad when I wouldn't sit in a chair.
No choice.

Stole money from Grandma, and she caught me.
Normal.

Mom took me to Florida for the summer. Next year we went camping with her boyfriend in Yellowstone Park.

She visited more often.

Two more friends in kindergarten. Irene and Cassie

My sixth birthday party. Grandma took us all to the zoo and gave us the dollhouse she had as a child.

I helped Grandma with the cooking. She loved that.

Good grades in the first grade. Mom and Grandma very happy.

Very independent, could take care of myself. Grandma liked that.

Summary for ages 4-6: I kept my friend Sal and I got more friends. I had good grades, I was independent. I was an angry kid and sometimes I broke things. Most of the trouble I got into was pretty normal. I helped my grandma and mostly I got along with my mother.

Ages 7-10

Evidence True

Burned lace tablecloth playing with matches—Grandma very angry.
Normal mischief.

Grandma went to live with my uncle. Mom said I was a hard child to raise when I went back to her.
She didn't know anything about parenting. That was the main problem.

Fighting with Mom; I was out all the time with my friends. Fighting over chores I was supposed to do.
Coping by escaping.

Hated Mom's boyfriend. He hated me because I took so much of her attention. We always competed.
Coping: He was taking attention I needed. I was scared they were just going to forget about me.

Evidence False

Mom said I was pretty and she loved my hair. Used to braid it.

Helped Grandma when she got sick (ages 9, 10).

Grandma said she would love me until she died and then from heaven.

I stayed tight with Irene and Cassie and then the twins, Adriana and Marta.

My science projects were the best in the class and my teacher seemed excited.

My mother read to me some nights and talked about her boyfriend. It felt close.

Billy Kittler took a big interest in me for a while.

My mother taught me how to swim.

Hated her other boyfriend. Screamed at him when he wouldn't stop car to let me go to the bathroom.
No choice.

Three girls picked on me the entire year in third grade. Made fart sounds when I walked by.
No choice.

Sal moved across town and he stopped visiting me (I couldn't go to his house).
No choice.

I was suspended from school for putting ink all over somebody's seat. Principal told Grandma I was a "problem child."
Coping: I think I was angry because I didn't believe my mother loved me.

We played around on her exercycle and laughed a lot (memory triggers tears).

Summary for ages 7-10: I lost Sal and I was picked on, but I got close to Adriana and Marta. Sometimes I felt very close to my Mom, even though we fought a lot. I was always trying to get her attention from her jerky boyfriends. I was angry frequently. It was how I coped with Mom not really being there.

Ages 11-15

Evidence True

Mom and I fought about my being late or never home. I was always with my friends.
Coping by escaping.

Tony dumped me because he was so constantly jealous.
No choice.

Boys had no real interest in me, just sex.
No one knew what a relationship was. It wasn't me. We were 13.

Cassie totally gave up her friends (me), to hang with guys.
She had to do it. I did it later myself.

Paying no attention to school. Mom super disgusted.
Coping: All my energy into friends so I wouldn't feel lonely and empty.

Mom marries Roger, and he comes on suddenly as a parent. We have these rages. He says I'm beyond help and out of control.
Standing up to Roger's abuse was a positive. I wouldn't let him run over me.

Evidence False

Still close to Irene and, to some extent, Adriana and Marta.

Visited Grandma a lot, long talks.

Tony really did love me for a while.

I'm fairly popular in the Stoner set (kids who do a lot of marijuana).

Mr. Collins really likes my diaries.

Mom still talks a lot about her problems, which kind of makes me feel good.

I'm always finding things to do for people, giving them little things, and I'm fairly well liked.

Wrote a short story about the Stoner scene which people liked. Particularly Mom.

Spent a few months living at Irene's. Her family liked me.

Summary for ages 11-15: I stayed close to Grandma, Irene, Adriana, and Marta, and I got close to Irene's mom. Tony was crazy jealous, but he did love me. Mom and I continued to fight, and it was the shits at school. But a lot of that was because I really was successful at keeping good friends (Cassie notwithstanding). People liked me. Even though Roger was disgusted with me, I'm glad that I fought him. He was a jerk. I wouldn't want him to like me.

Ages 16-20

Evidence True	*Evidence False*
Mom moved to Portland and I stayed here. It was like we'd gone on as long as we could and we'd just had enough of each other. *She'd done her best, I did my best, but the fighting was exhausting.*	Lawrence and I fell in love.
The slut thing at school. *No choice.*	Really felt close to Irene's mom.
The whole nightmare with my mom about Lawrence. The incredible bigotry. *No choice.*	Did OK at J.C. Got totally into physiology/nursing stuff. Direction finally.
Irene on me for deserting her. *Coping: Went for a relationship that really felt good.*	Lawrence wanted to live together.
	Knowing I could make it in nursing school. A big deal that I could do it.
	Letter from Mom.
	The trip to Yosemite with Adriana and Marta.

Summary for ages 16-20: The relationship with my mother stayed painful, climaxing in the huge blowout about Lawrence. But there was that weird letter asking my forgiveness. I was somewhat less close to my friends (although I'm still really close to Irene's

> mom). Mostly when I was twenty I felt really good about Lawrence and nursing school.

Full Summary

Up to now you've been making discrete summaries of each era in your childhood. You've been trying to weave together the evidence for and against your core belief into some kind of coherent whole. Notice how Arlene's summaries balance both the positive and negative memories. She wasn't Shirley Temple as a child, but she was a tough, gutsy kid who had good friends, was loved by her grandmother, and grew up without a lot of help.

The last step in the Historical Test requires that you put it all together, that you synthesize what you've learned down to some clear, basic truths about yourself. If you've done the exercises carefully, you'll find that this last summary will neither totally confirm nor totally refute your core belief. Like Arlene, you will be left somewhere in the middle. It isn't a black-and-white universe. That's extremely important to realize. Your core belief is probably true in some measure, but you have possibly discovered many ways in which it is *not* true. So rather than sticking to an absolute, unbending belief about yourself, you may now have an opportunity to see the exceptions, the balancing realities. Things may be less simple, less clear. But your new view of yourself may also be more accurate. Here's what Arlene said in her final summary:

> The whole belief that I'm not lovable was based on feeling Mom didn't love me. Grandma, Irene, and Cassie did. Adriana and Marta did. Even maybe Sal. Tony. And Irene's mom. Then there's Lawrence. It's clear that I've been loved. And Mom really was overwhelmed by me. She was too busy taking care of herself. After Grandma got sick, she was forced back into being a parent and was totally bad at it. I think she liked to talk to me and hang out. But she didn't want any problems. And I had problems. I was allergic. I was scared (wetting the bed), I lived in a

> dream world, I screwed up at school, I was kind of destructive as a kid and angry a lot later on. I just always felt that something was wrong, that Mom didn't want me or love me. So I guess I decided that I wasn't lovable at all. Which really seems to be a big exaggeration.

Let's take the case of Jeffrey, 47, who experiences a strong sense of being ashamed, unacceptable, and not belonging. Here is Jeffrey's Historical Test.

I'm Shameful, I'm Unacceptable, I Don't Belong

Ages 0-3

Evidence True	*Evidence False*
My father spanked me. I don't know about what.	

Ages 4-6

Evidence True	*Evidence False*
Summers in Maine. Just aimlessly walking around. No friends. Loitering inside certain stores. *Normal: Didn't know anybody. Shy.*	Saving my dog when he fell out of the boat (we shouldn't have had him in there to begin with).
Playing game of going up to the second floor and trying to get courage to jump. Not exactly to kill myself. But to do something daring or dangerous. And if I hurt	

myself, they would notice me, I guess.
Coping with loneliness.

First grade teacher putting me in a desk by myself because I talked all the time.
Coping with loneliness.

Summary for ages 4-6: I was just a lonely, isolated kid.

Ages 7-10

Evidence True

Hunting with my father. Not carrying the gun right. He's angry.
Normal.

He's angry because I won't fight and defend myself at school (this one kid kept extorting money from me). "Are you just going to lay down in life?"
No choice. Wasn't a fighter.

My father coming in angry after I left my bike out and it was stolen.
Normal forgetting.

My father teaching me how to use tools and getting angry when I used them wrong or sort of played with them.
Normal.

Evidence False

Playing with Steve.

Playing with Shrimp.

Getting along with all the teachers—a teacher's pet really.

Being a hall monitor at school (prestigious).

School play.

Shopping trips with my mother and sister. I loved that, and my father hated that I loved it.

Very good at singing. Used to sing for the family at parties (which my father thought was showing off).

"Showed butts" with some of the neighborhood kids.
I read that's normal.

When my father caught me giving away our fireworks to some of the kids. Many occasions like that of being slapped.
My father had an abusive temper. One-foot stimulus, ten-foot reaction.

Watching my mother undress and feeling something—maybe sexual. A kind of excitement. She didn't mind, but it felt shameful.

My father angry because I was spitting at the boats in the bathtub.
Normal.

> *Summary for ages 7-10:* I did great at school, I did have friends. I had a good relationship with my mother and sister. My father rejected me for things that were normal for my age. I spit in the tub, I left my bike out, I didn't like guns, I didn't like fighting. There was really nothing wrong with that, I guess. I do get a heavy feeling of shame about watching my mother undress.

Ages 11-15

Evidence True	*Evidence False*
Joined the football team and immediately got injured.	Hanging out with group at school that did plays.

Never played again.
No choice.

Constant masturbation, fantasies about confining women, abusing them, torturing them. (Very shameful.)
Read a lot about S&M, many people have these fantasies. It still doesn't feel "normal."

My sister walked in while I was masturbating. Terrified she would tell my father.

Sexual fantasies about mother (hugging, laying naked together).

After the divorce, my father visited infrequently. Nothing to say. Told him things about my plays. He didn't say anything, but I knew he disapproved.
He just had this prejudice about what a man should be. And it threatened him that his son wasn't really a man in his eyes.

Went hunting once with him. I didn't want to kill anything and felt ashamed. Kept missing every shot deliberately. He was obviously annoyed. So I finally did kill a bird.

Nice summer in Maine with my mother and sister.

Tagging along with my sister and her boyfriend, Chuck. I liked him. We used to play guitar together and work out some harmonies. (A sweet memory.)

Playing guitar and singing. Hanging out with a group at school that liked to sing rock and roll.

My mother and sister coming to my plays. Even Chuck came.

Most of my friends were girls. Didn't really fit with guys other than playing music with them. Felt close to Sharon and Barb, but upset that I sometimes had sadistic sexual fantasies even about people I liked. If I liked them, I wouldn't be doing the torturing, I'd watch someone else who was. And then sometimes the fantasies would involve saving them.

Hated myself for wanting his approval so much that I did it.
There's nothing wrong with not wanting to kill and also needing him to like me.

Had sex with two girls at school. Ashamed because I wasn't particularly attracted to them. Felt like I was cheating on one with the other. Also knew their families and somehow felt ashamed in front of them.
I was desperate to feel really close to someone and I thought sex would give that to me.

Felt like I wasn't real macho, I wasn't going to make it.
Normal, given what my father expected of me.

Summary for ages 11–15: Like before, I did great at school, I had friends (mostly girls now). I was in plays, I played music, I seemed to fit with groups that did that stuff. I still had a good relationship with my mother and sister and with Chuck. The shame mostly was around my father thinking I was sissified, unmanly. And sex. The feelings toward my mother (which were never sadistic). And the sadistic fantasies. They felt incredibly cruel and wrong.

Ages 16-20

Evidence True

Kept visualizing sadistic fantasies while having sex. Very shameful.

Told one girl a little about this, and she got upset.

Almost never saw my father. Always had the feeling that if he really knew me, he'd be disgusted—or maybe he did know me and that's why he stayed away.
I was the wrong kid for him, considering his values. It's not my fault that he had this very narrow idea about what a man was.

Relationship with Marjorie. Talking very rough and aggressively to her during sex.
Felt very wrong about it. I was trying to let out that part of me to see if anyone could accept it.

Kicked out of band for sleeping with drummer's girlfriend.
Coping: Kept using sex to feel close.

Evidence False

Got into two bands.

Relationship with Millie. Very sweet, not very turned on.

Went back to school to learn to be a surveyor. Liked being in school again, felt more like I belonged.

Joined a theater group. Had one of the lead roles in *Long Day's Journey.*

Friends with Jerry. Played gigs as Jeff and Jerry.

Lois. Very crazy. Very sexual. Kind of battered each other. But still very close at times. Shared fantasies with her.

Stayed friends with several ex-girlfriends.

Slept with other women while with Lois and felt ashamed about it.
Coping: Felt lonely even with Lois. Again kept trying to use sex to get close.

Summary for ages 16-20: Again the feeling that I was doing fine as far as school, acting, music, etc. It was this hidden underside of my life, this sense that I wasn't a real man, the man my father wanted me to be. But there was something worse. Sleeping with different women, feeling this need for closeness that I sensed only sex would give me. And sex getting me in trouble, particularly with Lois and the band. Mostly just feeling wrong about it. The closeness didn't seem to last anyway. The sadistic fantasies made me feel like there was something sick or corrupt inside of me. Like I was really screwed up. That's where the shame and feeling of being unacceptable seems centered. Like people would find out about that. Or my father would find out. He wouldn't like that stuff at all. Men protect women, that's what they do. I tried to expose this part of me and that helped. I look back at this exercise and, OK, the sexual stuff is there. It's a theme that runs through. It's one part of the whole picture. One part of my personality. My father wouldn't like it, but he hardly liked anything about me. This conviction that I'm unacceptable, that I don't belong, is mostly about him. I did well with lots of people. The sexual fantasies didn't stop me from liking women and having relationships.

Using the Historical Test

The Historical Test is a powerful way to examine and reinterpret parts of your life. In some cases, it will help you uncover memories. (Jeffrey had forgotten the sweet feeling of belonging when he went out with his sister and her boyfriend Chuck.)

The Historical Test may also permit you to contact positive feelings about yourself or others that are otherwise buried by a negative core belief. Jeffrey got in touch with his gratitude to Lois for letting him share some of his hidden sexual feelings with her. Arlene reexperienced her grandmother's kindness when she first came to live with her.

Don't expect to turn black to white. The Historical Test is designed to help you look for experiences that temper, soften, or shift your core belief from the extreme to a more comfortable middle ground. The point isn't so much to disprove your core belief, but to expand it to include other parts of your experience, to make it reflect realistically a fuller picture of yourself.

For each core belief examined by the Historical Test, try to distill what you've learned into a new statement of belief. Here are the "new beliefs" that Arlene and Jeffrey developed after finishing the exercise.

Arlene: A lot of people have loved me. My mother gave me as much love as she had, which wasn't enough.

Jeffrey: I wasn't acceptable to my father. But a lot of people in my life liked and accepted me. I still feel uncomfortable and somewhat ashamed about some of my sexual feelings. That's one part of me, but at this point it doesn't really get in the way of relationships.

5

Finding Testable Assumptions

Core beliefs are difficult to evaluate directly. They tend to be so global and generalized that proving or disproving them becomes a hopeless task. How can you absolutely prove or disprove a feeling that you are not safe in the world, or are not loved, or are incapable of independence? It's like trying to prove that Lyndon Johnson was tenderhearted, or that wasteful Americans get reincarnated as Untouchables. Who knows? It's impossible to get any hard facts.

Fortunately, there is a way to evaluate your core beliefs which doesn't involve tilting at windmills. Surrounding each core belief is a set of rules that require you to behave in specific ways. These rules are a blueprint for how you need to act in the world in order to avoid pain and catastrophe. They are a guide for which behaviors are OK and not OK, which are safe and which are dangerous, which are adaptive and which are disastrous. The rules generated by your core beliefs are testable, because implicit in each rule is a prediction of what will happen if the rule is broken. Behind each rule is a catastrophic assumption about how things will turn out if you ignore its mandate. You can therefore test your core beliefs by judiciously choosing certain rules to break and then comparing the outcome with the catastrophic prediction built into the rule. The following are some examples of core beliefs, the rules that flow from them, and the catastrophic predictions embedded in each rule.

Alexis

Areas of Concern and Core Beliefs

Others: People are deceitful, they're users, they leave you.

Performance: I don't know how to read people, to figure who's phony and who's genuine.

Rules and Catastrophic Consequences

1. Never express your pain, hope, feelings, or needs to friends. Keep conversation light or about neutral topics.

   Catastrophic Consequence (CC) for Breaking Rule: They'll get very uncomfortable because you're not fun. They won't "have time" to see you again.

2. Don't let people help you.

   CC: If you start depending on them, they'll let you down, they won't be around.

3. Don't trust men romantically; assume they are leaving; try to feel very little for them; don't count on them; stay very busy; see them infrequently. Never express affection, desire for more contact, or any emotional need.

   CC: They'll take you for granted, neglect you, abuse you. Or they'll feel suffocated and pull away. As soon as you really like them and depend on them, they've made their conquest and off they go.

4. Never be with people if you are sick.

   CC: They're only with you for a good time. They'll get uncomfortable, bored, etc. Then they'll leave.

5. Never admit mistakes.

   CC: People use the information to manipulate you, put you down, or write you off.

6. If there's a conflict in a relationship, get out of it.

   CC: You either have to acquiesce or they'll dump you.

Raymond

Area of Concern and Core Belief

Autonomy: I'll fall apart if I'm alone.

Rules and Catastrophic Consequences

1. Always travel with other people.

   CC: You'll be anxious, stressed. You'll be utterly alone, you won't meet anybody. It won't be fun.

2. Never leave a relationship. Hold onto it. Compromise, give in. Don't push too hard for changes and things you want. Don't fight or complain.

   CC: You'll feel anxious that they'll withdraw or pull out. The relationship will feel distant, lonely. You'll end up spending a lot of time alone.

3. Do what your friends want. Go along with things.

   CC: People don't like problems and conflicts. They'll stop inviting you places.

4. Talk about their lives, their interests, what they want to talk about.

   CC: They'll get bored and end up avoiding you otherwise. It'll be a loss.

5. Fill your time up on the weekends. Always have something to do at night.

   CC: You'll feel anxious, listless, you won't enjoy yourself, you'll feel too lousy to really relax or get anything done.

6. Never go to a party or become involved in a situation where you don't know anybody.

   CC: You'll be anxious, depressed, and you won't meet or talk to anybody.

Sandy

Areas of Concern and Core Beliefs

Justice: I'm a victim of a lot of unfairness.

Control: I can't protect myself.

Rules and Catastrophic Consequences

1. When people are angry or critical, get angry back.

   CC: If you don't, they'll just think they can abuse and push you around anytime they want. You'll get it more often.

2. Don't get into pleasing guys around sex.

   CC: Since they never pay any attention to what you want or what feels good to you, you'll feel angry and put off.

3. Don't do favors. Don't ask for things.

   CC: If you do favors, people won't reciprocate, and then you feel screwed. If you ask for something, then you'll be guilt-tripped and made to feel you owe them, or they won't do it and you'll feel hurt.

4. Always keep things exactly equal in a relationship.

CC: Because the guy will do less and less, give less and less, if you keep putting in the same energy. If he gives less, you give less.

5. Don't do extra at work.

   CC: They won't pay you, give you the promotion, etc. They'll just take as much as you'll give them.

6. Always have an ally.

   CC: You're an easier target if you're alone. They push more on you at work.

Morris

Area of Concern and Core Belief

Belonging: I don't fit anywhere, I'm not like other people.

Rules and Catastrophic Consequences

1. Don't tell people much about your feelings, things you like, things you do, things you believe.

   CC: They'll think you're weird. Things will feel awkward. They'll shun you.

2. Do things alone. Don't get involved in activities that require other people.

   CC: They won't want to include you or do things with you. You'll have to keep to yourself anyway. It'll be awkward and embarrassing.

3. Don't bother with women. They won't be attracted to you.

   CC: It'll be awkward. They'll be phony, make phony excuses, just another rejection.

4. Always be pleasant and polite, don't hassle people with your needs.

   CC: They'll get irritated, they'll treat you like a nuisance, an outsider.

5. Don't make waves at work, just do your job and go home.

   CC: You're an outsider, you're odd, you'll be the first to be fired.

6. Dress like everyone else.

   CC: If you dress camp or weird, they'll tag you as weird and write you off.

Erica

Areas of Concern and Core Beliefs

Security: I'm not safe.
Control: I'm not strong or able to take care of myself.

Rules and Catastrophic Consequences

1. Don't drive on the bridge.

   CC: You'll freak out, you'll freeze, you'll stop the car and have to walk.

2. Don't go to new places.

   CC: You'll be anxious, you won't enjoy anything, you'll keep wishing you were home.

3. Don't make friends with active, adventurous people.

   CC: They'll expect you to do things that are scary and they'll reject you if you say no.

4. Always know exactly what will happen and what to expect.

   CC: If you don't, you'll be freaked out. You won't be able to handle it (whatever "it" is).

5. Be sure you have lots of support and help for everything you do.

   CC: If you try to do something alone, you'll be overwhelmed and screw it up.

6. Steve (husband) has to pick you up at work.

   CC: If you drove yourself, you'd be freaked walking to the car.

Notice how in each example the catastrophic predictions make it very scary to break the rule. Since the rule is almost invariably followed, no one finds out if the assumed catastrophes really occur or are as painful as expected. And since the rules and catastrophic consequences go unquestioned and untested, the core belief remains impervious to challenge. Erica expects all her dire predictions to come true, and so she continues to view herself as weak and vulnerable. Morris assumes he will always be the odd man out. And because his predictions of being rejected go unchallenged, he can never find out where he fits and belongs. Alexis assumes that all people will use and mistreat her, and because her stark predictions go untested, she will never have the opportunity to experience trust.

Identifying Rules Derived From Your Core Beliefs

This exercise will help you to uncover the rules of behavior which grow out of any given core belief.

Step one: On the top of an 8½- by 11-inch sheet of paper, write down a core belief that you would like to explore and question. Ideally, this is a belief that you have identified as painful or life-restricting.

Step two: The quick list. Draw a vertical line down the middle of your paper and make your list in the left column. As quickly as you can, without giving it a lot of thought, write down everything that you should and should not do to protect yourself, given your belief. These are your "do's" and "don'ts" for surviving in the world and in relationships, considering the central belief you've just written down. Right now, on a piece of paper, write down everything that immediately comes to mind.

Step three: Basic rules checklist. Look carefully at each item on the following list. Ask yourself this question: If my core belief is true, what must I do or not do in this situation? Keep asking yourself what the rule is for each item on the list. Then add the rule to the left-hand column of your sheet.

Basic Rules Checklist

- Dealing with other people's...

  Anger
  Needs/desires/requests
  Disappointment/sadness
  Withdrawal
  Praise/support
  Criticism

- Dealing with mistakes
- Dealing with stress/problems/losses
- Risk taking/trying new things/challenges
- Conversation
- Expressing your...

Needs
Feelings
Opinions
Pain
Hope/wishes/dreams
Limits/saying no

- Asking for support/help
- Being...

    Alone
    With strangers
    With friends
    With family

- Trusting others
- Making friends

    Who to seek
    How to act

- Finding a sexual partner

    Who to seek
    How to act

- Ongoing romantic relationships
- Sex
- Work/career
- Dealing with children
- Health/illness
- Recreational activities
- Traveling
- Maintaining your environment/self-care

As you go down the basic rules checklist, it's important to be extremely honest with yourself. Don't whitewash things. Acknowledge openly how your core belief affects, even determines, your behavior for each item on the list. Ask yourself: "What do I really do to cope with my belief? How do I protect myself? What are my limits?"

To get an idea of how you can explore your rules, consider the case of Sonya. Here's how she did the exercise.

Core Belief: "I'm sensitive and vulnerable. I'm a coward." (Control)

Quick List: Sonja wrote these rules off the top of her head.

1. Don't get into fights.
2. Don't be around people who are upset — who've suffered a loss, who are in some kind of pain.
3. Avoid stressful challenges.
4. Don't go to any scary movies.
5. Avoid new or unusual kinds of sex.
6. Be very sweet to Ted (boyfriend).

Basic Rules Checklist: After the "quick list," Sonja examined each item on the Basic Rules Checklist and thought about how her core belief affected her in that situation. These are the additional rules she identified.

1. It's not good to be alone.

2. Stay away from Mom.
3. Don't get into heavy-duty problem solving. See if it goes away or someone can help.
4. Find friends who are strong and supportive, but won't push you around.
5. Don't push too much for what you want.
6. Keep things beautiful and aesthetically pleasing at home.

Generating Predictions

Now that you have uncovered the rules dictated by your core beliefs, it's time to link each rule to a specific catastrophic prediction. Go through your list of rules, and on the right-hand column of your page, make the catastrophic prediction that goes with each rule. Once again, the prediction is your picture of what will happen, the painful outcome, if you break the rule. The prediction should always contain specific, *objective* consequences: how others would behave, how you would behave, what would happen. You may also wish to include *subjective* consequences: how you would feel, what you would think. Sometimes you'll be tempted to write a consequence that only includes painful feelings. This isn't enough. Remember that you need *testable* predictions. It's a lot easier to verify objective events — what others did, what you did — than feelings. Feelings are influenced by suggestion. You tend to feel what you *expected* to feel. But observable behavior, real events in the world, are less subject to prior expectations.

The prediction is your fear talking. Listen to it. Really get in touch with what scares you about breaking each rule. Sometimes it's hard to admit that you are so influenced by fear. That's not at all unusual. There are good reasons for your fears. Somewhere in your past things happened that traumatized and hurt you. Your fears and rules are an adaptive effort to keep things like that from happening again. But now it's important to try to describe the fears, to give the nightmares sound and shape.

Don't be surprised if several different rules are supported by the same catastrophic prediction. It's quite usual for certain fear themes to show up again and again.

Here are the catastrophic consequences Sonya generated for each of her rules:

1. Don't get into fights.	CC: You'll be terrified and upset. You won't be able to stand the loudness and anger. You'll probably run away or completely break down in tears.
2. Don't be around people who are upset — who've suffered a loss, who are in some kind of pain.	CC: You'll end up overwhelmed with whatever they feel. You'll take it all inside, you won't be supportive or kind. You'll just have to get away.
3. Avoid stressful challenges.	CC: You'll be anxious, it won't be satisfying or exciting. You'll be too upset to do it right.
4. Don't go to any scary movies.	CC: You'll get overwhelmed and have to leave.
5. Avoid new or unusual kinds of sex.	CC: You'll feel incredibly awkward or weird. You'll do it wrong or want to stop in the middle. You'll feel molested. You'll make Ted angry by being cool and ambivalent.

6. Be very sweet to Ted.	CC: If he gets irritated at you, and you don't feel he's there as a buffer, a support, you'll get really anxious. If you're critical, he'll leave you.
7. It's not good to be alone.	CC: You'll feel anxious, you'll start compulsively calling people.
8. Stay away from Mom.	CC: You'll get angry and won't be able to control it. You'll blow up, and she'll hang up.
9. Don't get into heavy-duty problem solving. See if it goes away or someone can help.	CC: You'll mess it up, make problems worse, feel alone and overwhelmed.
10. Find friends who are strong and supportive, but won't push you around.	CC: You won't be able to push back if they try to control you. You'll tend to go along.
11. Don't push too much for what you want.	CC: If people get irritated with you, they won't really be there for support. They'll say no. You'll feel anxious and unable to count on them.
12. Keep things beautiful and aesthetically pleasing at home.	CC: Otherwise you'll feel less calm and relaxed. You'll get restless.

Identifying the Rules You Want To Test

There are five important guidelines for selecting rules to test:

1. Choose a rule where it's easy to set up a test situation. It should be something where you have control, where a simple change in your behavior puts the test in motion. It wouldn't make sense for Sonya to test her "Don't get into fights" rule, because fights tend to be spontaneous and depend partly on someone else's mood and behavior. "Find friends who are strong and supportive, but won't push you around" is also hard to test because Sonya would already have to know someone "pushy" and deliberately start to cultivate the relationship for the test to be set up.

2. Choose a rule that allows you to test the core belief directly. If Sonya can be supportive to a friend in crisis, it tends to undermine the belief that she's a sensitive coward. But deciding not to put flowers around her house to test "Keep things beautiful and aesthetically pleasing" probably won't have much impact on her core belief, however the test turns out. Raymond believed that he would "fall apart if alone," but testing his rule that he should do whatever friends want lest they stop inviting him to things won't have any impact on the core belief. All Raymond can find out is whether his friends can accept and enjoy someone assertive. The test still won't answer the question of what would happen after he's actually alone.

3. The rule should include a clear prediction of a behavioral response (yours and others), not just subjective feelings.

4. The outcome should be relatively immediate. For your initial tests, choose rules where the predicted consequence can be observed as soon as possible after breaking the rule. If you have to wait days or weeks to find out how things turn out, you'll lose your momentum for testing. Again, Sonya's rule about non-pushy friends, aside from not having a specific consequence, would probably take too long to test.

5. Choose a relatively low-fear rule to test. Or find a rule that could be tested in gradients, from only slightly scary to very scary. For example, the "Don't get into heavy-duty problem solving" rule could be tested incrementally. Sonya could make a list of problems and rank them from least to most difficult. Then she could choose a problem to work on from the low end of the range. Or with the "Stay away from Mom" rule, she could decide to speak to her mom for five minutes, maximum, on the phone, and in later tests increase the phone time. She could test the "Be sweet to Ted" rule by mentioning that leaving his stinky socks on the floor was a little irritating (low fear) and work up to more threatening communications like "You seem distracted and not there when we make love lately." Sonya doesn't have to start with explosive issues. By easing herself gradually into the forbidden waters of her negative feelings, she can test low-threat items until she has more confidence that the catastrophic predictions won't come true. If Sonya wants to test the "Avoid new or unusual kinds of sex" rule, she can mentally list the various sexual requests Ted has made and identify the one that is least anxiety-provoking. She may also set up the test so that Ted is told in advance that she is going to try something new, but needs full permission to stop if it really bothers her (thereby giving herself more control).

Raymond's belief that "It's not good to be alone" can also be tested in increments: one-half hour, one hour, two hours, one whole evening, and so on. Remember Erica, who was afraid of new places? She could practice going to new restaurants at gradually greater distances from home. Or try little day hikes in nearby parks she hasn't yet explored, then gradually work up to a two-day river rafting trip. Erica was also afraid of bridges. She could start by going over short, less threatening bridges. Or tackle the bigger ones with a friend for support. She could start driving the bridge with a friend next to her. The next time her friend could ride in the back seat out of sight. Then the friend could drive in a car right behind her, then five car-lengths behind her, then out of sight, and so on.

Hopefully you can now see how testing in gradients works — you divide the thing you are afraid to do into little steps, rank them from low to high fear, then test the smallest step.

This is the time to choose the rules you want to break and put to the test. Apply the five guidelines to your rules and choose no more than three rules that seem to fit the criteria. Break them down into gradients so you have an initial test that generates relatively low fear. The next chapter will provide guidelines for conducting your tests. But you have already achieved something very important. You've decided that your old, unquestioned core belief is really an hypothesis and open to question. You've chosen a concrete way to put it to the test, to find out once and for all if it is worthy of belief.

Sonya decided to test three of her rules:

1. "Don't be around people who are upset — who've suffered a loss, who are in some kind of pain." As it happened, her friend Marlene's mother had just had a stroke. Marlene was depressed. Sonya decided to make a brief call and monitor her reactions. Later, she might even visit Marlene.

2. "Avoid stressful challenges." Sonya made a list of things she sometimes wanted to try, but felt afraid to tackle. It went all the way from "find a new bookkeeper" (low fear) to "confront Ted's son about his drug problem and insist he enter a treatment program" (high fear). She decided the bookkeeper item wasn't quite challenging enough for her test, but confronting Ted's son was too threatening at this point. Instead, she focused on some middle-range items such as getting surgery on a small mole, setting limits with Ted's son about using the car, and telling her aunt she wasn't going home for the holidays (after last year's drunken debacle).

3. "Don't push too much for what you want." Here again, Sonya broke the rule into gradients. She made a list starting with "Ask Ted to help more with the dishes" (low fear) to "Tell Mom to please not call, I'll call her when I'm ready" (high fear). She decided to start with the dishes item and see how she did with that.

6

Testing Your Rules

You have been engaged in the work of the personal scientist. In the Historical Test, you systematically explored your past to uncover evidence for and against your core beliefs. Now it is time to explore your present life, to break selected rules you have lived by in order to test your expectations of a painful outcome.

A personal scientist attempts to apply the rules of science to self-exploration. This means making every effort to put aside your biases, fears, and assumptions in order to fairly test and objectively evaluate the data. Scientists aren't supposed to stack the deck. They're not supposed to manipulate their experiments so that an expected or desired outcome is inevitable. They aren't supposed to filter the data so that only certain facts are stressed, while others are buried.

The task of maintaining objectivity while exploring yourself is like trying to walk a straight line through a forest. You inevitably keep bumping into things. All you can do is continue trying for the general direction. As you test long-held rules of living, you may find yourself inadvertently acting in ways that promote the likelihood of a negative, catastrophic outcome. For example, Jill tested her rule against asking for things by making requests in a whiny, hostile voice. Or you may interpret ambiguous data through the lens of your core belief. When Jill's boss said he had to think about her request for a raise, Jill assumed that he was stalling because he didn't really value her work.

Attempting to be scientific means asking these two questions about each test:

1. Am I setting the test up fairly so it doesn't promote a negative outcome?
2. Am I being objective as I interpret the results?

The Testing Sequence

At the end of the last chapter, you chose up to three rules to test. Of the rules you decided to test, identify the one that, if proven wrong, would have the greatest impact on your core belief. Choose carefully. Testing a rule that you should always be polite probably won't have that much impact on a core belief of worthlessness. The test might even set you up to prove the core belief *right,* since being impolite often triggers a hostile response, and such a response might well give you the feeling that you aren't valued. Testing the rule that you shouldn't walk in the dangerous part of town at night isn't the best way to evaluate a belief that you can't protect or take care of yourself. If you survive the walk, you've only proven that you were lucky. If you get mugged, you've confirmed your core sense of helplessness.

At this point, you should be clear about which rule you first want to test. If you are, begin step one of the testing sequence.

1. **Identify one relatively low-risk situation in which to make your initial test** — choose a relationship or place that isn't too threatening. Make sure that this test is something that you are really willing to do. If you suspect that it isn't, look for a situation that evokes less anxiety.

2. **Write a specific, behavioral prediction of what the outcome will be, based on your core belief.** This is the hypothesis you are testing, an assumption that certain bad things will happen when you break the rule. The words *specific* and *behavioral* are important. Your prediction should be specific to the particular situation you are testing (how your sister will react when you tell her about feeling alone in your marriage), not a general assumption about what happens when you break a rule ("I'll get rejected if I tell anyone how I really feel"). Behavioral outcomes are predictions of what you or others will do and say. It's fine also to predict how you'll feel when testing a rule, but behavioral outcomes are an indispensable part of your testable hypotheses.

3. **Make a contract with yourself.** This means a firm commitment that you are going to break the rules on a specific day, in a specific situation. If you wish, you can strengthen your commitment by telling a lover, friend, or therapist about your plan. Ask for their support and agree to check in after the test to let them know what you learned.

4. **Script your new behavior.** Figure out in advance exactly what you plan to do or say. If you are testing a new pattern of communication, it's extremely important to examine your script for anything that could make your prediction a self-fulfilling prophecy. It is common that the expectation of rejection, anger, or embarrassment will affect how a person says things. You may find that your attempt at new communication sounds cold, angry, blaming, vague, obsequious, or contains some message that invites a negative response. And that negative reaction will appear to confirm your core belief.

   Therefore, as you script what you'll say, listen to the words for unintended nuances of meaning. Tape-record your script. Or rehearse it with a friend. Ask yourself how you sound. If you can, get feedback about whether you sound defensive, accusing, domineering, unclear, and so on.

Cedric had a rule forbidding him to say no to any sexual invitation from his girlfriend. He assumed that she'd get angry and imply that there was something wrong with him. When he scripted a new behavior to test the rule, Cedric didn't notice that his response sounded testy and annoyed ("I'm wiped out, this has been just too long a day") and his tone of voice was cold and distant. Fear had hardened his words and voice. It was his tone, not the refusal, that triggered the expected angry reaction: "What's with you? If you don't like a woman who can ask for it, say so." The next time Cedric tested his rule about saying no, he talked it through with a friend to get feedback.

5. **Test your new behavior and collect data.** On the same piece of paper where you wrote your negative predictions, note which, if any, of your predictions actually occurred. And note specifically what *didn't* occur.

   If the reactions of others to your test are ambiguous, you will need to ask them some questions.

   - Are you feeling OK about what I said?
   - Did you have any reaction to that?
   - How did that strike you?
   - I couldn't tell whether anything was going on for you when we talked about ___________.
   - I had the impression that you might be feeling __________ when I said ______________. Anything to that?
   - Is it OK with you that I _____________?

Note the answers down with the other data that you've collected.

6. **Select a second situation to test your rule, and repeat steps 2 through 5.** As you identify new situations in which to evaluate your rule, try to work toward increasingly more threatening (and therefore more meaningful) tests. The more catastrophic your predictions about breaking a rule, the more impact the test will have on your core belief if the prediction is not entirely borne out. Encountering few of the negative outcomes that you predicted during early tests will encourage you when taking on the tougher challenges.

When Raymond decided to break his rule about not spending weekend time alone, he began with a three-hour block on Saturday afternoon. He took a long walk on the beach, and felt surprisingly little of the anxiety and restlessness he had expected. His success encouraged him to try a five-hour block, and then an entire day by himself. Eventually, he felt enough confidence to tackle another rule, this one forbidding traveling alone. He started with a day trip to Marine World and eventually worked his way up to a four-day camping vacation. On a cold October evening, in a nearly deserted campground, Raymond came to the startling realization that he *enjoyed* extended time alone. It was his mother who thought that being alone was tantamount to death. Like most children, he had simply believed her.

Predictions Log

Developed by Christine Padesky (Beck, Freeman, and Associates 1989)

The predictions and test data you have started writing down are the beginning of a *Predictions Log*. This is an extremely important tool for evaluating your core beliefs. It's your version of a scientist's lab book. It will help you record and *remember* your "observations." After you have performed a number of tests for a particular rule, you'll find it helpful to go back and review what you've learned. Does the rule still seem valid? Or should you change it to account for what you have observed.

In some cases, you may end up testing a rule in many situations or with many people. Consider Gertrude's rule that you can't ask for things or people will respond with irritation and withdrawal. In fourteen situations over the past month, Gertrude found that eleven people were relatively cooperative with her requests and three seemed annoyed. As a result of literally tallying her observations, she is now beginning to live in a much less black-and-white world. Instead of assuming she'll be rebuffed, she sees things in percentages. About 20 percent of people show irritation, but 80 percent seem to think that it's OK for her to ask for things.

The Case of Sony—Continued

Perhaps you remember Sonya from the last chapter. She saw herself as sensitive, vulnerable, and a coward — and therefore incapable of dealing with basic life problems.

Of the three rules that Sonya originally decided to test, "Avoid stressful challenges" seemed the most important. Her sense of herself as weak and afraid and therefore incapable of controlling her life could be examined most directly by breaking the "stressful challenges" rule. Here are the steps of Sonya's testing sequence.

1. **Identify one low-risk situation.** Sonya decided to tell Ted's son, Mark, that he could no longer use her car.

2. **Write a specific, behavioral prediction.** "Mark will get angry and blast me; Ted will be upset that there's a big beef; I'll feel anxious and extremely disturbed about my relationship to both of them."

3. **Make a contract with yourself.** Sonya decided to tell Mark her decision on Monday afternoon, when just the two of them were in the house together. She told a friend about her plan and promised to report on how it went.

When Monday rolled around, Sonya knew she wouldn't feel like doing it. But she decided to commit herself to the test, no matter how she felt.

4. **Script your new behavior.** "Mark, because you've been unreliable about getting the car back to me on time, and frankly because I know you drink heavily on dates, I've decided not to let you use my car in the future."

When she looked her words over, they sounded cold and accusing. And when she role-played her script with a friend, her friend noticed that Sonja's voice had a hard, almost contemptuous quality. Sonya realized that confronting Mark was so anxiety-provoking that she was pumping herself up with anger. And it was a very real possibility that her cold, dismissing anger would trigger in Mark the very reaction she feared. Sonya revised her script and role-played it again:

> Mark, it's been hard for me to decide this. But I've gotten really concerned about your sometimes drinking and driving on dates. It's also bothered me when I haven't gotten my car back when I wanted to use it. So for the time being, I'm not going to lend you my car.

Sonya's friend suggested that she open with a new line: "Mark, I've decided something that I hope won't be a major problem between us." And Sonya decided to finish with: "I've decided for the time being not to lend you my car. The problem with the drinking on dates and sometimes getting it back very late has me really concerned. I'm sorry about this." If Mark objected or started arguing with her, Sonya decided to use the "broken record" strategy. She'd just repeat her basic point in slightly different words, talking slowly and calmly.

In reviewing her script, the tone now seemed right, and Sonya felt ready for her Monday encounter with Mark.

5. **Test and collect data.** Here are the notes from Sonya's Predictions Log:

> Mark was calm and kind of flippant. "OK, if that's the way you want it. I don't drink more than anybody else." He sort of hurried out of the room. When I told Ted, he congratulated me on the decision and said he was thinking of doing the same thing himself. I do feel somewhat anxious about what will happen between Mark and myself. I suspect things will be very cold, but somehow that feels tolerable. Basically, my prediction was *very* inaccurate.

Sonja followed up by going on to step 6 and selecting a second situation: she decided to go ahead with getting surgery on a small mole. Her catastrophic prediction was that she'd be extremely nervous with anticipation. She'd be "out of it" (meaning extremely distracted and uncomfortable) with Ted and at work. She thought she might have an anxiety attack in the waiting room before the procedure. After the surgery, Sonya wrote the following in her Predictions Log:

> I thought often about it during the week, but I could still concentrate and still enjoy Ted. I wasn't "out of it." I was tense in the waiting room, and my voice was very tight while he prepared the Novocaine. But no anxiety attack. I was more capable of dealing with the stress than I predicted.

Next, Sonya decided to tell her aunt she wasn't going home for the holidays. Her aunt was upset and guilt-tripped her, but Sonja had surprisingly little reaction when she got off the phone.

After several other challenges, Sonya felt ready to tackle something that was high stress: confronting Mark about his drug problem and need for treatment. Since she and Ted had swept this one under the carpet, Sonya decided that she wanted Ted's support in facing the situation. She asked him to join her in confronting Mark. Together, they worked on the script, refining it until what they said was clear but not punitive. Sonya also took on the task of researching in-patient treatment programs for teenagers. They decided in advance which ones seemed best for Mark.

Just as Sonya predicted, the confrontation became extremely volatile. Mark slammed out of the house. Sonya and Ted decided that Mark couldn't continue to live with them unless he first went through treatment. Over the next few days, they kept repeating this message to Mark. Mark reacted by setting the Christmas tree on fire, dumping garbage on the kitchen floor, and smashing his collection of porcelain liquor bottles. It was a nightmare. But within a week, he did go into treatment. All of Sonya's behavioral predictions had come true. What hadn't come true was her collapse. She continued to feel surprisingly strong and clear. She and Ted had both been scared, but it felt like they were committed to seeing it through. In the middle of an emotional volcano, Sonya was amazed at her fiber, her willingness and ability to handle pain.

With Mark in treatment, Sonya had time to read back over her Prediction Log. She tallied up the score. In six challenging situations, she hadn't been overwhelmed and she hadn't collapsed emotionally. Even when her aunt and Mark reacted with the anger she predicted, she had felt much less vulnerable than she expected.

Look for Opportunities To Test

As you continue to test, begin looking for spontaneous opportunities to break old rules. Try things you used to avoid. Expand your focus to additional rules you wish to test. Be vigilant for any situation in which you can try new behavior. Over time, scripting your behavior ahead of time will become less and less formal, and eventually unnecessary.

Inevitably, you will have setbacks. Someone will reject you, you'll feel scared, uncomfortable, hurt, and so on. Sometimes your negative predictions *will* come true. Often they will not. Many times some component of the catastrophic prediction will be borne out, while others will simply never materialize. Keep track of what you learn in your Predictions Log. This data you are gathering is essential to your goal of expanding and correcting your core beliefs.

Rewriting Core Beliefs

After a period of testing and data collection, it's important to see if you can synthesize what you're learning. How does the data impact your core beliefs? Does it suggest ways you should revise your assumptions?

It's time for an update. Try to rewrite the core belief so that it incorporates the results of your tests. Identify exceptions to your core belief. Note anything in the belief that has turned out to be simply false. Include balancing realities — things you've learned about yourself that mitigate or soften the old negative self-portrait.

Sonya rewrote her core belief as follows: "I have more courage and ability to face things than I thought. I really can handle problems — from surgery to my guilt-tripping aunt to Mark's incredible rage when we confronted him. I have a surprising amount of strength."

7

Strengthening New Core Beliefs

In this chapter you will elaborate your revised core belief statements into a new set of rules to live by. You'll keep a log of experiences that tend to support your revised beliefs and rules. And you'll learn how to act on your new beliefs in more and more areas of your life.

New Rules From New Core Beliefs

At the top of a blank sheet of paper, write your revised core belief statements from the previous chapter. For these new core beliefs, write a new set of rules implied by the beliefs. Look back at the chapter on finding testable assumptions, get out your old list of rules, and revise them.

Put your new rules in the form of affirmations about yourself. Write them in the first person: "I can ask for what I want" instead of "You can ask for what you want." Keep your affirmations short, simple, and positive. Positive means "I share my feelings" instead of "I don't hide my feelings," or "I trust Jack but not George" instead of "Don't trust anybody."

Stick to the present tense, not the future: "I accept challenges" rather than "I will accept challenges." Wherever possible, include a prediction of logical consequences for each rule. This is where you can use the future tense. For example, "I can ask my Mom to watch the kids — she will let me know if it becomes too hard for her."

Don't worry if you don't feel entirely comfortable with or convinced of these statements at this time. Your goal is to elaborate a complete, very positive list of self-statements surrounding your new beliefs.

Here is an example of Alexis's revised core belief statements and rules:

Old core beliefs	*Revised core beliefs*
Others: People are deceitful, they're users, they leave you.	Others: Some people can be trusted. They are decent and will stick by me.
Performance: I don't know how to read people, to figure out who's phony and who's genuine.	Performance: I can figure out who's phony and who's genuine by trusting them and seeing what happens. I can learn to be a better judge of people.

Old rules	*New rules*
1. Never express your pain, hope, feelings, or needs to friends.	1. I sometimes share my feelings and needs with old friends: it brings us closer.
2. Don't let people help you.	2. I can accept help from people, especially Denny and Marguerite: they'll make good on their promises, and it doesn't mean I'm dependent.

3. Don't trust men romantically; assume they're leaving...never express affection, desire for more contact, or any emotional need.	3. It's OK to be affectionate with men and ask for affection from them. If I assume they're staying and give them cause to stay, they often will stay.
4. Never admit mistakes. People use the information to manipulate you.	4. I can admit mistakes and go on to something new. People will think better of me for acknowledging my mistakes than for trying to hide them.
5. If there's conflict in a relationship, get out of it.	5. I can ride out conflict in a relationship, I can negotiate for what I want without leaving or giving in.

Alexis noticed that the small, cautious shift she had made in her core beliefs resulted in a huge change in her rules for how to act with other people. This is a common experience of the power of core belief work: there is a kind of psychological leverage at work whereby slight modifications of belief can empower sweeping behavioral change. It's as if each core belief were a powerful searchlight in the center of a vast, dark plain. Shifting the searchlight a quarter of an inch to the left or right illuminates miles and miles of new terrain.

Don't be surprised if you read over your list of new rules and they sound like they belong to an entirely different person. There's no reason to be anxious or discouraged, either. Right now your new rules are bound to sound foreign, and you don't have to adopt them all at once. You can gather some more evidence first.

Keeping an Evidence Log

With your new beliefs and rules clearly articulated, you can begin to review your day-to-day experience and see if events bear you out.

Keep your log simple. Start with a sheet of paper divided into two columns:

What happened	*What it means*

On the left, record interactions with others, events, observations of others, mistakes, how you handled stresses, conversations, experiences by yourself — anything that supports your revised core beliefs and the new rules surrounding them.

On the right, note *how* these experiences support your new beliefs and rules.

Here's a page from Alexis's log:

What happened	*What it means*
Denny helped me clean out the back yard.	Accepted help, got it as planned, worked out fine, don't feel dependent on Denny.
Marguerite returned the $40 she borrowed last summer.	I'd kissed that money goodbye, and here it is.
Bob called me after our date, just like he said he would — wants to play tennis Saturday. I said OK, I'd be glad to.	I can start to trust him, let him know I enjoy his company and welcome more of it.
Told my sister about feeling afraid of her anger. She said, "Ali, I can't believe you're being this open with me."	I'm becoming more trusting.

Guessed who dunnit on Mystery Theater on TV.	Maybe I'm a better judge of character than I thought.
Saw a teenage boy flirting with a girl at the bus stop and didn't think, "Watch out, honey."	I don't have to assume that everybody's a hustler.

It's hard to remember to keep such a log. You're likely to forget to make notations or to put off making them until you can't remember everything that's happened to you. If you have such trouble, try some of these tricks:

- Review recent events for evidence of your new core beliefs every time you start your car, pick up your purse, flush the toilet, do the dishes, look in a mirror, and so on. To remind yourself, put some colored tape on the mirror, toilet, car keys, or your watch, to cue the review process. You might also set your watch or a kitchen timer to go off every two or three hours as a reminder to review your most recent experience.
- Set aside time each day to write in your log: before getting out of bed, after lunch, during your coffee breaks, before bed, and so on. Make your log a part of your routine, like brushing your teeth.
- Each time you interact with someone, take a moment to review what was said, for some evidence of your revised beliefs or that you are acting according to your new rules.

Choose Your Arena

To make your new core beliefs an integral part of your identity, it's not enough to passively sit back and collect evidence. You need to take action. You need to make things happen.

This can be very frightening and confusing. It's one thing to perform intellectual experiments and come to the rational conclusion that you need to shift your negative core beliefs to a more positive position. It's another thing to actually operate in your life as if you believe in your own competence, safety, worth, and so on.

The way to make things happen is to do it in one circumscribed area of your life. You need to choose a single arena in which you will perform "as if" all your new beliefs were entirely true and integrated into your personality (Kelly 1955, 1963).

An arena can be a particular person, place, setting, or time. For example, you can choose to act according to your new rules only with your mother, only at work, only in a classroom setting, or only on Thursdays.

For your first arena, pick an area of your life in which you feel relatively safe. Don't try to tackle your most intense relationship or the responsibilities that you find most stressful. Look for a clearly defined part of your life in which you have a pretty high degree of control, with ample opportunities to put your new beliefs and rules into action.

For example, Alexis was going through a divorce, living on her own in a new apartment, taking classes in computer programming at night, and working as a word processor for a local hospital during the day. She was under a lot of stress in her relationship with her husband, at school, and at work. So for her first arena, she chose a low-stress relationship — her dealings with her new landlady.

Her landlady was a good choice because Alexis didn't have much history with her. She could make a fresh start. Also, Alexis had an easier time dealing with women than men, and she wasn't home all that much, so her contact with the landlady could be minimized and controlled.

Script Your New Routine

Approach this task as if you were writing a character description and a script for a scene in a movie or a play. Look first at your revised core belief statements and list of new rules. Which of the new rules apply to the arena you have chosen? How do your new guidelines suggest you act in the particular relationship, place, or time you have marked for change?

Write down the applicable rules, and then elaborate them by describing how you would act in this situation or with this person if you really were more convinced of your own worth and competence, more trusting of others, more secure, more in control, or feeling more lovable, independent, comfortable, and so on.

Imagine the next time you will be at work, with your friend, home alone on Thursdays, or whatever. Actually write down what you plan to do, to say, to wear. You can also practice saying the important things out loud in front of a mirror to get your phrasing, tone of voice, gestures, and facial expressions just right.

Don't worry about feeling phony or artificial. It's natural to think, "This isn't me. This will never work." Remember, you just have to act "as if" you are a different person for a short time, in a carefully chosen setting.

When you have the whole script or description of the scene written, lie down and close your eyes. Breathe very slowly and deeply for a couple of minutes to get relaxed. Then run through the upcoming scene in your mind, playing it out in full color and detail, just the way you want it to go. At first, watch yourself as if you are in a movie, hearing what you say and seeing what you do. Then run through the scene from your own point of view, imagining that you are actually saying and doing everything. This kind of role-playing in your imagination will be a great help in making you more comfortable when you actually go on to put your new beliefs into action.

Alexis' script went like this:

Rules that apply to Doris (her landlady):

1. It's OK to accept any help she offers. Don't assume she'll renege.
2. Admit any mistakes — like tell her about the broken shower rod.

3. Share my feelings.
4. Ask for what I want.
5. If there's conflict, negotiate instead of running away.

OK, I'm really a person who can like and trust people. I can count on my own judgment about people. Doris seems perfectly nice and reasonable so far. I should assume she will stay that way. I should take her at face value. I consider her a potential friend and ally, not an adversary. I can seek her out, not wait till the rent is due or she wants something from me.

Here's the scene: Instead of feeling guilty about the broken shower rod and agonizing about it and putting it off, I use the rod situation as an icebreaker, an opportunity to get to know my landlady. I'm secure, I have nothing to fear. I call her up. I'm dialing the phone. I say, "Doris, how are you?" She says, Fine, what's up?"

I say, "Listen, I have a little problem with my shower rod. Can you come up sometime soon and look at it?" No, I say, "Why don't you come up for a cup of coffee this morning, and we can figure out how to fix it."

She says OK, she'll be up in half an hour. I'm casual, in jeans and a shirt. But my hair is brushed, I'm looking like a wholesome, healthy, quiet person — the perfect tenant. The apartment is clean and neat — not obsessively spotless, but it looks nice. I'm obviously taking care of the place.

Doris comes to the door. I open it, smile, say "Hi, how are you doing?" Big hearty voice, exuding cheerfulness and trust. I pour coffee and we sit down at the kitchen table. I tell her how much I like the apartment. It's quiet, cozy. I ask her how long she's been here. Show interest in her, what she's like.

> Share feelings. Tell her I'm a little nervous living here alone. Tell her that I'm getting a divorce, under stress, feeling lonely. No big confession, just matter of fact, open and available. She offers sympathy, tells me something about her own life — doesn't matter what.
>
> Bring up the curtain rod. Say that I also have been feeling guilty. Admit mistake: "I lost my balance in the tub, grabbed the rod, and it pulled right out of the wall. Come on, I'll show you."
>
> We go in the bathroom. She looks at it. Says whatever she says about how she usually fixes things. I offer to pay for it — cheerfully, matter of fact, not guarded and suspicious. We're new neighbors, not foes.
>
> We agree on what we'll do. We part on good terms. That's the goal: establish a real relationship, not get hung up in ducking blame for the rod or on suspicions that she's going to rip me off or hate me.

Alexis practiced this scene in her imagination twice. She stood in front of the bathroom mirror and actually rehearsed the hard parts about revealing her feelings and owning up to the broken shower rod.

Act As If Your New Core Beliefs Are True

Now go out and actually do it. In your chosen arena, act as if you were your new self — more confident, secure, safe, competent, and so on. Follow your script as closely as you can, acting as if your new rules were second nature.

It will help to repeat your rules to yourself while you're operating in your chosen arena. Use them like affirmations or slogans to remind you of your new ways of being in the world:

"I can figure out what I want and need. I can say no. I can protect myself. I am a competent human being," and so on.

Critique your first attempt at acting "as if." What worked? What didn't work? What felt natural and easy? What felt phony and difficult? What was the outcome? How did the other person react? How did you feel afterward? What did you tell yourself while it was going on?

Based on your review, alter your script. Put in more of what worked and change what didn't work. Refine and enlarge your character — the new you. Plan your next encounter just as you did the first.

It's like being in a play in which you're the playwright, director, and star. You write a scene, block it out, walk it through, critique it, and start again — revising, trying new gestures and staging, reviewing the results, taking it from the top over and over until it "plays" as natural, comfortable, powerful, and inevitable.

When Alexis actually invited Doris up to her apartment, it went fairly well. But she was very nervous. They were drinking coffee at the kitchen table as planned, but Alexis had a hard time working her feelings into the conversation. She managed to say, in a quiet, strangled voice, "I like it fine here, but it's nervous and alone sometimes" — not at all like the smooth, natural admission she had rehearsed. But Doris didn't seem to think it sounded weird. She was actually quite sympathetic.

When they got to the bathroom, Alexis found it very hard to take the blame for wrecking the curtain rod. She wanted to blame the slipperiness of the tub and the flimsiness of the curtain rod for the whole thing. But she bit her tongue and just said, "I'm really sorry this happened, and I'm willing to pay whatever's reasonable to get it fixed." Doris said it would only be a few dollars and that she'd have someone come up to fix it on Friday.

When she was leaving, Doris said, "I notice you need some curtains up here. I have some in the basement that an old tenant left. They'll fit these windows, and you're welcome to them if you want them." Alexis stifled her automatic tendency to turn down help. She said sure, she'd like to look them over.

Alexis reviewed the encounter later and was pleased. She planned to rehearse talking about her feelings more before her next encounter with Doris. To help herself stick to her plan, she had lunch with her friend Marguerite and told her what she was trying out with her landlady. She said, "Marguerite, you've got to hold me to it. I'm going to get together with her again and look at some old curtains she's got. And no matter how ugly they are, I'm going to graciously accept them and thank her sincerely. And I'm going to tell her about the time I sewed curtains with my Mom and what a nitpicker she was. I want to call you next Tuesday night to tell you how it went."

Alexis went down to the basement with Doris to look at the curtains. They were a little faded, but she thanked her landlady and carefully folded them to take upstairs. She told Doris how she had made curtains with her mother as a young girl, and how hard she tried to get it right, and how much it hurt her feelings when her mother pointed out Alexis's mistakes.

While she was talking about her mother, Alexis felt a few moments of ease. She suddenly slipped completely into character, and it seemed like she was just talking freely with a friend, not repeating lines she had memorized. She got a sense of what it was like to be the kind of person who could just let her feelings flow out without worrying about the audience's reception.

In time Alexis and Doris became friendly. Alexis began to look forward to taking the rent check downstairs each month. They shared many cups of coffee, chatted while they did their laundry, and picked up small items for each other at the grocery store. Her relationship with her landlady became a source of real satisfaction, instead of the antagonistic tug-of-war she had expected.

Expand Into New Arenas

When you are comfortable and have had some success following your new rules in the first arena, expand into another area of your life. If you have done well with your mother, tackle your brother next. If you can successfully conduct a Thursday evening at home alone, how about an entire Saturday on your own? If you have become comfortable dealing with people in stores and gas stations, try the same tactics with the people in your aerobics class.

Each time you move into another arena, review your list of new rules and revise your script. Retain what works and is beginning to feel natural and pleasant. Add new guidelines to cope with new complexities. You can expect to feel awkward and artificial all over again when you are acting "as if" in a new situation or with new people. Continue the process of scripting, acting "as if," reviewing, and revising, until you feel comfortable following your new rules in each new arena.

For Alexis, the next arena was her friend Marguerite. She had already asked for her support in dealing with the landlady, so it was fairly easy to continue to open up with her. In this case, Alexis was able to "come clean" about what she was up to. She told her friend that she was working on trusting people more and learning how to share more of her own feelings, ask for what she wanted, accept help, and so on. Marguerite was glad to help by being a "guinea pig."

Alexis really knew she was making progress when she came down with the flu and was able to ask Marguerite for help. Her old pattern was to hide out when she was sick, not contacting anyone because "nobody wants to be around sick people." This time she asked Marguerite to pick up her paycheck and take it to the bank, turn in her term project at school, and take her cat to the vet. She felt very proud of herself for being able to reach out for help when she wasn't feeling good.

Alexis went on to make an ally of an instructor at school, finalize her divorce without feeling too much like a victim, and pursue a long-term relationship with her old tennis buddy, Bob. Eventually she found herself telling relative strangers things like "You've got to trust certain people, take that chance. If you don't, you end up scared and alone. Sometimes you get burned, but that's a necessary risk."

When she caught herself expressing her new beliefs spontaneously, without a script in mind, Alexis knew that the "as if" phase was coming to an end.

And that's what happens. "As if" becomes "because." Where once you took risks *as if* you were deserving and confident, eventually you will take risks routinely *because* you *are* deserving and confident. It sounds like magic, but you really do become what you pretend to be.

There's an expression concerning physical health that says "You are what you eat." Where mental health is concerned, the equivalent sayings might be "You only see what you look for," "You believe what you see," and "You become what you do." The deceptively simple truth is that belief is a skill. It's a skill that you learn by doing. It's a skill that can make you a conscious molder — not a prisoner — of belief.

8

Visualizing Core Beliefs

Psychologically speaking, it is not true that you can't change the past. Although you can't alter what happened to you or what you did, you can use visualization to restructure your memories so that they cause you less pain and interfere less with your present life.

In this chapter, you'll return to the historical material you explored in chapter 4. With careful planning, you'll be able to revisit painful childhood scenes armed with new, more positive core beliefs. The visualization methods you'll learn in this chapter can actually change the impact of those early scenes on your adult identity.

You can begin working on this chapter before you have completed all the exercises in the previous chapter. Visualization will make strengthening your revised core beliefs easier.

Your Inner Child

Your unconscious mind doesn't believe in time. To your unconscious mind, things that happened when you were six months old can be just as important and immediate as things that happened yesterday. Deep inside, your entire infant personality survives in every detail. This inner child has no knowledge of any older versions of you. It is an infant with an infant's needs, abilities, and understanding of the world.

Likewise, you have a two-year-old toddler inside you, with a two-year-old's self-centered and contrary feelings. There are countless versions of you, of all ages from birth to your present age.

The inner child is more than an interesting metaphor. It explains why people act "childishly," or "immaturely." It's because some stressful event reminds them of a childhood trauma and awakens a younger version of themselves. They react as if they were still two or five or ten years old.

Painful feelings that you experienced as a child and never resolved return to haunt you in the form of negative core beliefs about yourself. Unmet needs from early times still drive you to this day.

In the past few years, techniques have been developed for "reparenting your inner child" to resolve old painful feelings and meet old needs symbolically. This work is often done in twelve-step recovery programs by adult children of alcoholics or by victims of childhood sexual or physical abuse. These powerful techniques also work very well for those who struggle with negative core beliefs.

This is the basic idea: you imagine that you, a wise, experienced adult, are visiting yourself as a child during a particularly hard time — a specific scene that you have already identified as contributing to one of your negative beliefs about yourself. You impart to your younger self the wisdom you have acquired and the skills you later developed to deal with hard times. Specifically, you counter the negative belief that is being formed with a more positive, more accurate version. You actually become, in your imagination, the perfect parent and friend that you needed at the time but didn't have.

Your unconscious mind doesn't believe in reality any more than it does time. That is, it doesn't distinguish between actual experience and dreams or fantasies. The good advice and support that you give your inner child in your imagination, years after the fact, can be processed and stored and used by your unconscious just as if it had really happened. The fact that you have two contradictory versions of the same memory doesn't bother your unconscious, because it doesn't insist that things make logical sense.

Visiting your inner child is a two-way street. You go back in time to bring your child the experience, wisdom, and strength that you lacked at the time to understand the world and protect yourself. And your inner child comes forward in time to return to you the spontaneity, creativity, and pure joy of living that you had to suppress in order to survive as an adult.

1. Translate New Beliefs Into Messages for Your Inner Child

Take the new, revised core beliefs you developed in the previous chapter, examine them, and if necessary translate them into short, simple positive messages that you can deliver to your younger selves.

At the same time, figure out at which age you needed to hear these messages. The exercise that follows is broken down into different ages that correspond to major stages of normal child development. Different core beliefs tend to be formed at different stages of development. But no two people's experience is identical. The following breakdown (Bradshaw 1990) is meant to be just a rough guideline to what to look for at different ages — not a rigid outline that you must follow.

Infancy — Your First Year

During your first year, you're totally dependent on your parents, especially your mother, for the food, warmth, care, and love you need to thrive. So the core beliefs likely to be influenced by your earliest experiences will probably be concerned with love and security. If these are problem areas for you, you might compose messages like this:

You are safe and secure.

You are lovable and precious.

You can trust me to take care of you.

There is enough love and nurturing for you in the world.

Write here what you'd like to say to yourself as an infant:

____

____

Toddlerhood — 1 to 3 Years

Toddlers are literally learning to stand on their own two feet and explore their new world. The core beliefs most likely to be rooted in these years have to do with autonomy and value. Here are some examples of empowering messages to your inner toddler:

You can stand on your own two feet.

I love your curiosity.

You are a unique, valuable person.

It's OK to say no.

Write your messages to your toddler here:

____

____

Preschool Age — 4 to 6 Years

From ages four to six many core beliefs are formed, especially in the area of performance or competence. Here are some examples of things you might tell yourself as a preschooler:

You do many things well.

You can learn to do anything.

Every day you're getting better and better.

Write your message to your preschool self here:

____

____

School Age — 7 to 10 Years

During this time, the issues most likely to come up might concern control and personal standards. Here are some possible messages:

You can be in control of your life.

You are responsible for your own behavior.

I like how you make a plan and follow it.

You set reasonable rules for yourself.

Write your own special message to your school-age self:

____

____

Adolescence — 11 to 15 Years

This is a troubled time for most people, a time when any of the developmental concerns can be recapitulated. Unmet childhood needs and unresolved feelings can return to haunt you. In addition, you might have had trouble with concepts of belonging and justice. Here are just a few of many possible messages for your troubled adolescent self:

You fit in well with your good friends.

It's OK to feel confused.

You can accept not getting what you want.

You can handle it when life seems unfair.

Spend some time composing positive core beliefs to pass on to the adolescent inside you:

____

____

Young Adulthood — 16 to 20 years

By now, the suggested time frames may be quite out of phase with your own development. That's OK. You are your own person, with your own developmental pace. By the time you are a young adult, most of your core beliefs have been formed. The issues that face a young adult concern finding a stable love relationship outside your family of origin, plus coming to grips with work — what you are going to do in life. How you view the essential nature of other people becomes very important at this time. Here are some typical core belief statements that others have found useful:

Others are doing the best they can.

Everybody's just trying to survive.

Most people will give you a break.

Write here what you plan to say to yourself as a young adult:

____

____

2. Get Very Relaxed

Being completely relaxed is almost like being hypnotized. It makes it easier to concentrate fully and makes you more open to suggestions. It's the essential first step for all visualization exercises. When you're relaxed, you can form more detailed and intense mental images and get the most out of the time spent visualizing your inner child.

Besides, relaxation training is therapeutic in itself. When your body is relaxed, your mind is relaxed. Your most negative and distressing beliefs are robbed of their power when you are profoundly relaxed. It is literally impossible to be uptight when your muscles are loose and relaxed.

Lie down in a comfortable position with your arms and legs uncrossed. Close your eyes gently. Clench your right fist, making it tighter and tighter. Study the tension in your fist. Notice as you keep it clenched that the tension is in your fist, wrist, and forearm. After five seconds, relax your arm. Feel the relaxation in your right hand and notice the contrast with what it felt like before. Concentrate on this feeling of warm relaxation for about fifteen seconds. The secret of this progressive muscle relaxation method is to learn what muscle tension feels like so you can learn what relaxation feels like.

Repeat once, clenching your right fist again for five seconds, then relaxing it for fifteen seconds. Then do the same with your left fist twice. Finally, do both fists at once, tensing and relaxing.

Next, bend your elbows and tense your biceps, both arms at once. After five seconds of studying the tension, relax and let your arms fall to your sides. Notice the feelings of relaxation for about fifteen seconds. Repeat this once again.

Now wrinkle your forehead. Frown as mightily as you can for five seconds. Then let your face go smooth for fifteen seconds, feeling the relaxation. Frown again and relax. Next, squint your eyes tightly shut, then relax them until they're just lightly closed. Move on to your mouth by clenching your jaw — not too hard, there's no need to crack a tooth. Feel the tension in your jaw. This is where many people habitually store tension, unconsciously pressing or grinding their teeth together. Let your jaw relax and your mouth hang slightly open. Feel the relaxation. Repeat the tensing and relaxing of your jaw muscles. Try pressing your tongue upwards next and feel that tension. Relax. Purse your lips in an *O* and relax them.

Push your head back as far as it can comfortably go and notice the tension this puts on your neck. This is another chronically tight set of muscles. Roll your head to the sides and to the front, noticing how this changes the tension. Then relax your neck muscles, let your head come to rest, and feel a warm flood of relaxation.

Shrug your shoulders up as high as they will go. Feel the tension for about five seconds and let your shoulders droop. Study the feeling of calm and looseness. Your entire body is starting to relax. Take a deep slow breath and fill your lungs completely. Hold your breath and see how this produces a feeling of tension in your chest. Let the air out slowly as you settle more deeply into relaxation. Repeat this deep breathing several times, settling more deeply into relaxation with each exhalation.

Skip this next part if you have back trouble. Arch your back slightly and feel the tension. Then release and relax. Repeat.

Tighten your buttocks and press your heels down against the floor to tighten your thighs. Hold and then relax. Then try curling your toes downward to tense your calf muscles. Do this slowly so you won't develop a cramp. Stop if any cramping begins. Relax your calves and feel warmth and heaviness taking over your legs. Now try to draw your toes upward, putting tension into your shins. Hold and release.

Lie there quietly, breathing slowly, and scan your entire body. Feel the relaxation moving upward, from your legs and trunk to your shoulders, arms, and head. If any parts of your body still feel tense, go back to them and repeat the tense-relax cycle until stiff muscles relax and go limp.

3. Visualize Your Infant Child

When you are completely relaxed, you can start visualizing your inner child, beginning with yourself as an infant. This can be a very powerful, emotional experience. If you begin to feel overwhelmed by your feelings at any time during this exercise, you should open your eyes and stop at once. Don't continue until you have talked it over with someone. If you have a history of serious mental illness, and especially if you were physically, sexually, or emotionally abused as a child, you should consult with a mental health professional before doing inner child work.

A good way to do these visualization exercises is to read them onto a tape. Speak slowly and clearly, with frequent pauses. Rephrase the instructions so that they apply to your unique circumstances and include the things you plan to say to your inner child.

As you're sitting or lying there, feeling very relaxed and heavy and warm, imagine that your body is expanding into the air or sinking into the ground. Your body is merging with the universe. You are encompassing the whole world. The whole world, all space and time, is taken within you. You become the whole world or the whole universe. Feel your present consciousness as a spark or flame at the center of the vastness of your own history.

Imagine that within you is a parklike landscape, with paths, woods, meadows, buildings, streams, and fountains. Within this park you can find all the times of your life, all the selves that you have been at all ages and in all places. Your inner world contains all that has ever happened to you and all that you have ever thought or dreamed about.

Imagine that you are standing on a path in your park. Look down and study the surface of the path. Look at the color and texture, the little pebbles and tufts of grass. Hear birds singing and the breeze whispering through the trees. Smell the clean scents of fresh air and green growing things. Feel the wind caress your face, and your skin glowing warm under the sunshine. This is your special place, your inner world that you can make any way you want. You are in control here. You are in charge.

Start walking down the path. This path cuts through time. You can visit any time of your past just by strolling along this path. As you saunter along, you notice a structure off in the distance. As you approach, notice that it is the house or apartment or trailer or whatever that you lived in when you were born. If you never actually have seen the home of your birth, just make it up to look any way that seems right.

Enter the home and go to the room where you slept as an infant. Again, if you don't know what it really looked like, that's OK. Make it any way you want. Notice the door to the room. Is it wood? What color is it? Open it and go in. Find a crib or bed. Go to it and see a sleeping baby. This is you as an infant. Study your tiny fingers, your little mouth, your wispy baby hair. Notice the color and texture of the blanket. What kind of diaper or sleeper does the baby have on? The more details you add, the more real this moment will become for you.

Now imagine that your infant child wakes up and starts crying. Really hear the wails of protest. It gets louder and louder. Now see your mother, father, or whoever took care of you coming in. They can't see the adult you. You're like a ghost or a disembodied observer — the proverbial fly on the wall.

Watch your mother or other caretaker coping poorly with your needs — being cross and angry, being rough or not cuddling your infant self, trying to feed you when you really need to be changed, trying to change you when you just want company, and so on. See and hear your infant self fretting and fussing.

Now have your mother or whoever leave the room. Your infant self starts crying again. This time, go to your infant self and pick the baby up. Cuddle and hug your infant self. Give some milk from a bottle.

Talk to your infant self as the crying stops and is replaced by calm and contentment. Say what you have prepared to say to yourself as an infant. Also say some of the following messages, in your own words:

Welcome to the world.

I'm glad you're here.

I'm glad you are a girl (or boy).

There's never been anyone else exactly like you before.

I love you.

I love you just the way you are.

I'll never leave you.

I'm going to take care of everything you need.

You're just acting normally for your age.

You have no real choices to make right now.

You're doing the best you can to survive.

Hug your infant self one more time and put the baby down. Say goodbye and promise to return soon. Turn and leave the room.

Now you need to change your point of view. You're going to run through this scene again, but this time you will actually be your infant self. Actually imagine that you are very tiny again. You're lying in your crib, just waking up. As you come out of that warm fog, you begin to feel bad. You're hungry. You want something warm to fill you up and enfold you. You want your mother. Imagine that you are lying helpless in that crib, unable to do anything for yourself, hungry, cold, wet, lonely. You cry and cry.

Imagine your mother or other caregiver coming in, not giving you everything you need at this moment. She or he leaves, and you still aren't filled up.

Now imagine your future self leaning over your crib and smiling down at you. Notice what your future self is wearing, how the hair is fixed. You can see yourself as a wise old wizard or sorceress, or you can have your older self look just as you really look. Pick a comforting, trustworthy image.

Feel yourself being picked up, hugged, cuddled, and talked to. Hear all the messages over again and know that they are for you: you are welcome to the earth, you are loved, your needs will be met, you are unique, you are just the right gender, you are perfectly normal for your age. You don't have to be hungry or cold or lonely again. You can count on your future self, your ideal parent, to always be there.

Hear your future self saying goodby and promising to return. Go back to sleep knowing that you are loved and cared for.

Now get ready to end the visualization. Become your adult self again and leave your first home. Stroll down the path to a comfortable place to lie down. Close your imaginary eyes and know that when you open them, they will be your real eyes. It will be now and you will be your present self again, in the real world. Remind yourself of your immediate surroundings. Count to three slowly, and on the count of three open your eyes and get up carefully. Think back over your visualization experience and tell yourself you did a good job. You have made a good start. You feel refreshed and renewed.

This is a good visualization to repeat any time you're feeling overwhelmed, helpless, or insecure.

4. Visualize Your Toddler Inner Child

In this second visualization, follow the relaxation induction until you are very relaxed. Once again, imagine that your boundaries are expanding and that you are sinking down within yourself, to that magic inner world.

Find yourself once again on the path that leads to your inner child. This time, spend a few moments fixing details in your mind: the smells, sights, sounds, and tactile feelings of your inner world. Notice what kind of trees there are and what kind of soil is underfoot. Notice what you're wearing — your regular clothes, wizard robes, a special hat or jacket, or whatever makes you comfortable.

Stroll down the path until you come to the place you lived when you were two or three years old. Enter your toddler home and look around. Check out the kitchen, see some of your favorite toys lying around, notice any of the furniture you remember. If details are hazy from real memory, make something up that is plausible.

Now you are going to visualize one of the earliest scenes you can remember. Pick a time that you identified in chapter 4 while performing the Historical Test. Pick a time when you were unhappy, when something happened that hurt. It can be an actual memory or based on a story your family later told you about your early years. If you get some of the details wrong, it won't matter. The exercise will still work.

See yourself in the situation. How are you dressed? What color is your hair? How long is it? Notice the expression on the face of your inner toddler child.

Watch the painful scene begin — when you broke something, when someone abandoned you, when something was taken away, when you were spanked or scolded. See how upset your inner child becomes. Concentrate on the details — the sights, sounds, smells, tastes, and tactile feelings.

When the scene is over, take your toddler self aside, into another room or some other safe place. Introduce yourself. Say: "I am you. I'm from the future when you're all grown up. I've come to help you, to be with you whenever you need me."

Tell your inner child what you have planned to say at this stage. Also tell your toddler self:

> I love you.
>
> There's never been another kid like you.
>
> I like you just the way you are.
>
> I'll never leave you.
>
> You're acting normally for a child your age.
>
> It's not your fault — you have no choice in the matter.
>
> You're doing the best you can to survive this hard time.
>
> It's perfectly all right to explore.
>
> I'll protect you while you learn about the world.
>
> I love taking care of you.
>
> You have a right to say no.
>
> It's OK to be angry or scared or sad or afraid.
>
> I can meet your needs.

I love watching you grow up and become your own person.

Hug your younger self and say goodbye. Promise to return whenever needed. Turn and leave the room.

Now switch your point of view. Become yourself at age two or three. Relive the scene you just witnessed, but this time actually imagine that it's happening to you again. Really feel the pain. Without the real feeling, there won't be real healing. Feel how frustrated you were when you didn't get your way. Feel how curious you were as a toddler. Experience the mingled fear and love you feel for the adults around you. Sense the shame of feeling responsible for the anger and upset that surrounded your attempts to understand the world.

When the hard time is over, see your future self come into the room. This wise, gentle, loving figure from your future is the experienced, powerful, wise being you will become. Actually see all the details of your future self. Hear all the messages of love and support that you need to hear at this vulnerable time of your life. Hug your future self and know that you can draw on this super figure any time you feel threatened or confused.

Say goodbye. Lie down and close your imaginary eyes. Know that when you wake up you will be in the present again, grown up and working on your core beliefs.

Remind yourself of your present surroundings. Tell yourself, "When I get up, I'll feel like a weight has been lifted. I'll carry some of my magical child wonder around with me the rest of the day." Open your eyes on the count of three. Stretch, get up, and go about your usual routine, noticing your world with fresh eyes.

You should repeat this toddler visualizatio—to cover all the significant painful scenes you can remember from this very early period in your life, inserting positive core belief statements in place of early negative formulations. This is a good exercise to do whenever you are feeling confused, abandoned, put down, or shamed.

5. Visualize Your Preschool Inner Child

Prepare the messages you have planned to deliver to yourself at ages four through six. Review your notes from the Historical Test. Pick the first memory you want to relive.

Get very relaxed in a quiet place and once again sink into your inner world. Explore the path back through time until you come to your home, the place you lived when you were four or five or six, before you entered first grade.

Spin out the memory scene you have chosen. First, pay attention to your preschool self. Watch without being seen. How tall are you? Skinny or plump? What are you wearing? Are there any favorite toys around? What color are your eyes? How is your skin tone? Are you fresh and rosy from a bath or hot and dusty from playing outdoors? Make up a complete picture of yourself, including the little details that make fantasy seem real: the grime under your little fingernails, the bandaid on a scraped knee, the special barrette you wore right on the tiptop of your head to make a topknot like Woody Woodpecker's.

Watch the scene — the fight with your cousin, the scary time daddy came home drunk, the time your mom just lost it and got hysterical, the time you got lost at the county fair, the time that the bully at daycare threatened or attacked you. Notice how scared or confused your preschool self is. Notice how your inner child tries to understand and make things right, even though the skills and knowledge aren't available.

When it's all over, take your inner child to a safe place and sit down together. Tell your younger self that you are visiting from the future, that you can be the kind, attentive parent that is missing, and that your younger self can count on you. Tell your preschool self the messages you have prepared. If anything else that seems important comes to mind, say that too. Put your arm around your inner child and say:

> I love you.
>
> I'm glad you're a boy (or a girl).

> You're the only one like you in the world, and I like you just the way you are.
>
> You're doing your very best right now.
>
> You just don't have much power to change what's going on.
>
> You're acting normally for a kid your age.
>
> I'll help you figure out how to protect yourself.
>
> It's OK to cry.
>
> You're good at thinking for yourself.
>
> You're good at imagining things.
>
> I'll help you separate what's real from what's imaginary.
>
> It's good to discover the consequences of what you do.
>
> You can ask for what you want.
>
> You are not to blame for your mom's and dad's problems.
>
> It's OK to ask me any questions.

Try to sense how your inner child is interpreting the event. What does the *child* believe is going on? What does it mean to the child about his or her worth, lovability, safety, belonging, and so on? The child is confused and trying to make sense of things. Offer an explanation to your inner child that leaves him or her innocent and blameless for what happened. If there is a positive way to interpret the child's behavior, offer that now.

Now change your point of view and relive the painful scene, this time as if you were four or five or six years old. Really experience the shame, the anger, the confusion, the fear. Remember, without the feeling you won't get the full benefit of the visualization.

At the end of the painful experience, see your future self arrive like a savior. Go with your future self into a safe place and hear all the comforting, important messages. You feel safe, important, all right. Pick two or three of your future self's statements that are particularly fitting and encouraging and repeat them to yourself.

This next part is a new step that you haven't done before. Relive the painful scene once again. This time, experience it as if you know your future self and *already* understand the positive messages your future self has given. You will know this time what you didn't know before: that it's all going to turn out OK, that you will survive, that it's not your fault, and so on.

This time, feel less pain in the scene. If it feels right, you can change the memory and react differently than you did in real life. For example, if you were lost at the fair, instead of sitting down and crying, you might find an adult and ask for help. Or if you were scared and alone in your room, listening to your parents fighting, you might imagine yourself singing songs to drown out their words.

Whatever you do, don't blame yourself for not reacting differently at the time. You really were doing the best you could. Also, don't change the actions of others in your scene. Even in imagination it's important to remember that you can't change other people's behavior, only your own.

After you have experienced the painful scene with less unhappiness than in real life, change your point of view again. Become your future self and say goodbye. Tell your preschool self that you will be back. Give a hug and remind the preschooler that he or she can draw upon your experience any time.

Return along the path of time. Lie down and close your imaginary eyes. Remind yourself of your actual surroundings, count to three, and open your real eyes. Get up and tell yourself, "I did well. I am actually restructuring my memories."

Repeat this preschool visualization for all the problematic memories you have identified from this period in your life. This is a good exercise to repeat whenever you are feeling dependent, ashamed, or guilty.

6. Visualize Your School-Age Inner Child

This visualization follows the same pattern as the previous one. Get relaxed and imagine a scene from ages seven through ten: the time you were humiliated in front of the whole second grade, the time your father didn't show up for the school play, the time you were made to feel stupid or clumsy or inadequate. Relive the painful memory, first from the point of view of your future self.

At the end of the scene, take your school-age self aside. Tell yourself the belief statements that you have prepared. Also cover these topics:

The way you are at school is OK.

I'll stand up for you.

It's fine to try out new ideas and ways of doing things.

You can make your own decisions.

It's OK to disagree.

You can trust your feelings.

It's OK to be afraid.

We can talk about anything.

You can choose your own friends.

How you dress is your business.

You're acting normally for your age.

You have no real choice in this matter — there's nothing else you could do.

You are doing the best you can to survive.

As you did with your child during the last visit, try to sense how your inner child is interpreting the event. Understand what it means to your child in terms of his or her lovability, control, safety, and so on. Again, offer an explanation that leaves your inner child innocent and blameless for the event. And if there is a positive way to interpret the child's behavior, offer that here.

Then repeat the scene two more times, first from the point of view of your school-age self, feeling all the old painful feelings but having the help and support of your future self at the end of the scene. Finally, relive the scene as your school-age self but with your future skills and knowledge. The last time through, you can change how you reacted in the scene if you want.

End the exercise as you have done before, and tell yourself, "I am bringing my inner child to life, I am renewing myself."

Repeat this exercise for all the school-age memories that you have identified as contributing to negative core beliefs. This is a good visualization to use whenever you are feeling discouraged about your own competence.

7. Visualize Your Adolescent Inner Child

This visualization follows the previous one step for step. This time, get relaxed, enter your past, and visit a painful event from your adolescence, roughly ages eleven through fifteen. For most people, this is an era with plenty of pain to choose from — rebellion against parents, conflicts at school, intense and stormy peer relationships, new and powerful sexual feelings, and so on.

First observe, from your adult point of view, the memory you have chosen. Then take your adolescent self into a safe place and share the adult, reasonable beliefs you have prepared. Also explain the following in your own words:

> You can find the right person to love.
>
> You can find something meaningful to do in life.

It's OK to disagree with your parents.

You are becoming an independent person.

You can safely experiment with sex.

It's OK to feel confused and lonely.

You have lots of new and exciting ideas about life.

It's OK to be wrapped up in yourself now.

It's normal to be ambivalent.

It's all right to feel embarrassed and awkward.

It's fine to masturbate.

No matter how far out you go, I'll be here for you.

You're acting normally for your age.

Often you have no real choice in the matter.

You're doing the best you can to survive.

Again, offer an explanation that leaves your child blameless for the events. Look for a positive way to interpret the adolescent's behavior.

As before, relive the scene from your adolescent point of view twice: once to feel the original pain with your future self there, and once as an adolescent with your future skills and knowledge, perhaps changing your behavior from what actually happened.

Return to your future self, say goodbye, and return to the present. Repeat this exercise to heal all the painful memories you have earmarked from your adolescent years. You can return to your adolescent inner child any time, especially if you are feeling confused about sex or in conflict with authority.

8. Visualize Your Young-Adult Inner Child

Following the same steps as in the last exercise, visit a painful scene from your young adulthood. After viewing the scene, confer with your young-adult self and convey the positive beliefs you have formulated. Also put the following in your own words:

> You will learn how to love and be loved.
>
> I know you will make a difference in the world.
>
> You can be a success on your own terms.
>
> You're acting normally for your age.
>
> You're doing the best you can to survive.
>
> Often you have no choice in the matter.

Again, offer an explanation for the events that casts your young-adult self in a compassionate light. Look for a positive way to interpret your young-adult behavior.

Then experience the hard time from your young-adult point of view, with all the frustration and pain you can remember, but with your future self there to help. Finish by reliving the scene again as your young-adult self, but with your future skills and knowledge. Let yourself act differently if you wish.

Return to your future self and say goodbye. Come back to the present knowing that you can handle adult life on your own terms. Revisit scenes from your young-adult life until you have healed all the memories that have contributed to negative core beliefs. This is a good exercise to repeat any time you have those familiar feelings of confusion over work, money, or love.

Lucy

Lucy was a daycare provider who was working on core beliefs regarding her own incompetence and lack of power. She used visualization extensively to heal wounds in her early childhood and adolescence. Out of over 25 visualized visits to her past, two were especially effective and meaningful.

Lucy's feelings of incompetence dated back to her preschool years, when she was five years old. A particularly painful memory was the time a hotpad caught on fire while she was trying to make a cup of hot chocolate "all by herself." To prepare for visualizing this memory, Lucy prepared three messages that she needed to hear at the time:

> You're not bad.
>
> All five-year-olds do this stuff.
>
> You can learn to do things all by yourself.

To begin her visualization, Lucy laid down on her couch and spent five minutes relaxing every muscle in her body. She then imagined that her flesh was turning to sand, crumbling and merging with the warm sand of a beach. She became the beach, then the ocean, then the mountains. She expanded to be one with the whole world.

Lucy took a walk in her imagined interior world, hiking up a hill, into a forest, and coming to a clearing in which stood the house she lived in as a preschooler. She entered the house and went to the kitchen. She saw herself, five years old, getting the little aluminum pot, getting the milk from the fridge, pouring the milk carefully into the pot. She concentrated on details, like the way she stuck her tongue in the corner of her mouth and bit it to help her concentrate on not spilling the milk.

She filled in the sound of the stool scraping over the floor as her preschool self dragged it over to the stove. The little girl looked over her shoulder nervously. Her mother was in the back bedroom, changing her little brother's diapers. She wasn't supposed to touch the stove, but she wanted to show how she could make hot chocolate all by herself.

Lucy watched her young self put the pot of milk on the front burner, then turn on the back burner by mistake...the burner with the hotpad on it! She watched in horror as her younger self, too short to reach the burning hotpad and too frightened to think of turning off the burner, screamed "Mommy, Mommy!"

Her mother rushed in, grabbed her off the stool, flung her toward the living room, shut off the burner, scooped the hotpad into the sink, and ran water over it. She was yelling the whole time:

"What the hell are you doing? You little brat, I told you never never touch the stove. What's the matter with you? Can't you ever do anything right?"

Lucy watched her mother force the crying preschool kid back into the living room, trap her up against the couch, grab her shoulders, and begin shaking and shaking, screaming and screaming. She saw that both mother and daughter were hysterical.

Then she heard her baby brother crying in the back room. her mother slammed the little girl down on the couch and left the room. "Don't you move a muscle. Stay here."

Then Lucy entered the scene as her future, adult self. She sat next to her crying, preschool self and put her arm around the little girl.

"It's all right," she said. "You're not bad. All five-year-olds do this stuff. You can learn to do things all by yourself."

Lucy realized that, at five years old, she had felt that she deserved her mother's anger and rough treatment. She had felt that she really was a bad girl, a defective kid who never did anything right. Now, from her adult perspective, Lucy was able to offer a kinder interpretation:

> Your Mommy's really more scared than mad. She's afraid you might have been burned. But she never had time to tell you about her fears. She's so busy taking care of you and Jimmy by herself that she makes mistakes. It's not your fault. You're just doing the best you can. It's good to try to do things for yourself. I love the way you are growing up.

Lucy replayed the whole scene again, imagining this time that she was five years old and that it was happening all over. She really felt the pain, the guilt, the confusion...and the relief of being comforted by her future self. She loved hearing "It's not your fault," and "You can learn to do things all by yourself."

The other memory that Lucy succeeded in restructuring was an experience from her adolescence, when she was very depressed about having moved away from her high school friends and not having any close friends at her new school.

She visualized a typical afternoon after school: waiting for her mother to get home from work, alone in the dim living room of their new apartment, curled up in an overstuffed chair, watching a teen dance show on TV and crying. She visualized her future, adult self joining her adolescent self, sitting on the arm of the chair, rubbing the girl's thin shoulders, and delivering the message from the future:

> Lucy, I've come back again to tell you that things will get better. You have very little control over where your Mom wants you to live, but that doesn't mean it will always be that way. Next year you will meet a really good friend named Marcia. You'll have a blast together and barely remember your sophomore year. You need to know that you will survive this loneliness and powerlessness. You can learn to take control of your life and reach out to find new friends.

When she replayed the scene as her adolescent self, Lucy imagined that she knew she would survive. She deviated in her imagination from what usually happened on those long afternoons: she turned off the TV and started doing homework, a rare behavior for her in that time of her life. It represented taking control by doing something positive.

Conclusion

Have you ever seen one of those Russian doll sets that fits inside each other? You take the top half off the biggest doll and there's a slightly smaller doll inside. Then you take the second doll apart and there's an even smaller doll inside that. And so on, and so on, until you reach a tiny infant doll at the core. Your inner children are like that—a succession of younger versions of yourself, complete and fully formed, hidden inside, yet there any time you choose to look.

As John Bradshaw suggests in *Homecoming,* you can visualize all your inner children at once, like a family reunion. You should be able to do it with ease if you have worked through each step so far. Gather in your interior park for a picnic. Let your young adult pick up and cradle your infant self. Watch your adolescent self making sandwiches for your toddler and preschool selves. Play a game of tag with your school-age self. Imagining these playful scenes is a great way to relax and just have fun.

All your early selves can be a source of energy and inspiration for you here in the present. They bring back to you the joy, spontaneity, and creativity that you may have had to stifle on the way to becoming a serious adult.

To remind you of this, and to make your visualizations more vivid, try collecting pictures of yourself at various ages. Put them up where you'll see them every day.

You can also write letters to yourself, repeating the positive belief statements used in the visualizations. Writing these statements out in longhand is a good reinforcement. It gets your body involved, helps you to slow down and pay attention to every word, and makes a stronger impression on your mind.

9

Keeping It Together

If you've actively worked many of the exercises in this book, and taken each step in the process of examining your core beliefs, you've accomplished a great deal. And it's taken time — several months or more. Your perception of yourself has shifted. Your self-portrait is recognizable, but to some degree altered.

Now comes the last step — consolidating and protecting your gains. With time, old negative beliefs tend to slip back into consciousness. Your new self-portrait may begin to smudge and take on more of the old likeness. When artists finish a sketch, they protect it by applying a matte finish. It's important for you to do the same thing psychologically. You need a way to protect and maintain your new perspective.

Core Belief Summaries

Buy a stack of 4 by 6 file cards. Label the top of each card with a particular area of belief that you have tested or examined historically — safety, worth, competence, and so on. Don't bother making cards for belief areas you have not investigated. Now go back over the summaries you developed in the Historical Test. Write down on the file cards any evidence that feels compelling in support of your new, more positive beliefs in each area. Or any convincing evidence that contradicts the old belief. Also, glean from the summaries some of the more general statements about how you now see yourself: "It's clear I've been loved." Or "I did great at school, I did have friends, I had a good relationship with my mother and sister. My father was screwed up and rejected me for things that were perfectly normal behavior for my age."

Now go back to the Predictions Log, where you recorded outcomes as you tested your rules. Write on the appropriate file card either specific events or summaries of your findings that support your more positive core beliefs. Also include events and findings that cast doubt on the old negative beliefs.

At the end of the testing process, you were asked to rewrite your core beliefs. Include on your file cards any convincing statements that you generated during that process.

Finally, check your Evidence Log to identify important *new* experiences that support your revised core beliefs. Enter these on the appropriate file card.

Now, in each significant area of belief, you have compiled important statements that remind you of your changed self-portrait. For the forseeable future, you should make a habit, even a discipline, of reading one of your file cards each day. And when you have read the last card, just start over again.

Also commit yourself to reading the appropriate summaries when you experience negative emotions. If you feel depressed or anxious or guilty, read the evidence for your new core beliefs. It can have a very powerful effect, bringing back into focus your new self-portrait.

Every day of his life, a Roman Catholic priest is required to say an "office." He reads from a little book the prayers that remind him of his role, his work, and his identity. You have worked hard to shape a new, more positive, more accurate identity. Like the priest, you will need to say your "office," to remind yourself of who you have become. It is a small daily task, but one that will allow you to take what you have gained into the years to come. The core beliefs summary, and all the effort you put into it, is your key to the prison of belief. It will open the door to a freer, more fulfilling life.

Bibliography

Beck, A., J. Rush, S. Hollon, and B. Shaw. *Cognitive Therapy of Depression*. New York: Guilford Press, 1979.

____________, and G. Emery. *Anxiety Disorders and Phobias: A Cognitive Perspective*. New York: Guilford Press, 1985.

____________, A. Freeman, and Associates. *Cognitive Therapy of Personality Disorders*. New York: Guilford Press, 1990.

Bradshaw, J. *Homecoming*. New York: Bantam, 1990.

Fanning, P. *Visualization for Change*. Oakland, California: New Harbinger Publications, Inc., 1988.

Freeman, A., J. Pretzer, B. Fleming, and K.M. Simon. *Clinical Applications of Cognitive Therapy*. New York: Plenum, 1990.

Guidano, V.F., and G. Liotti. *Cognitive Processes and Emotional Disorders*. New York: Guilford Press, 1983.

Kelly, G.A. *The Psychology of Personal Constructs*. New York: W.W. Norton, 1955.

____________. *A Theory of Personality*. New York: W.W. Norton, 1963.

McKay, M., M. Davis, and P. Fanning. *Thoughts and Feelings: The Art of Cognitive Stress Intervention*. Oakland, California: New Harbinger Publications, 1981.

____________, and P. Fanning. *Self-Esteem*. Oakland, California: New Harbinger Publications, 1987.

Meichenbaum, D. "Cognitive behavior modification with adults." Workshop for the First Annual Conference on Advances in the Cognitive Therapies: Helping People Change. San Francisco: April 1988.

Padesky, C. "Advanced cognitive therapy of depression." Workshop for Advances in Cognitive Therapies: Helping People Change. Long Beach: September 1989.

____________. "Personality disorders: Cognitive therapy into the 90's." Paper presented at the Second International Conference on Cognitive Psychotherapy, Uned, Sweden: September 18-20, 1986.

Raimy, V. *Misunderstanding of the Self: Cognitive Psychotherapy and the Misconception Hypothesis.* San Francisco: Jossey Bass, 1975.

Segal, Z. "Appraisal of the self-schema: Construct in cognitive models of depression." *Psychological Bulletin.* 1988, 103:147-162.

Young, J. *Cognitive Therapy for Personality Disorders: A Schema-Focused Approach.* Sarasota, Florida: Professional Resource Exchange, Inc., 1990.